LEX CROUCHER

YOU'RE CRUSHING IT!

Positivity for living your **REAL** life

BLOOMSBURY
LONDON OXFORD NEW YORK NEW DELHI SYDNEY

BLOOMSBURY YA
Bloomsbury Publishing Plc
50 Bedford Square, London, WC1B 3DP, UK

BLOOMSBURY, BLOOMSBURY YA and the Diana logo
are trademarks of Bloomsbury Publishing Plc

First published in Great Britain 2019 by Bloomsbury Publishing

ISBN: PB: 978-1-4088-9247-3; eBook: 9871-1-5266-1324-0

2 4 6 8 10 9 7 5 3 1

Typeset by Janene Spencer
Printed and bound in Great Britain by CPI (UK) Ltd, Croydon CR0 4YY

To find out more about our authors and books visit www.bloomsbury.com
and sign up for our newsletters

This book is dedicated to my friends for having my back and my front, my family for giving me far too much confidence in myself, my cat for standing on the keyboard and deleting most of my manuscript multiple times, and to my boyfriend, unless we've broken up, in which case it's dedicated to my next boyfriend.

CONTENTS

MENTAL HEALTH AND BODY IMAGE RESOURCES (UK)

Mind

Provides information on a range of topics including: types of mental health problems; where to get help; medication and alternative treatments; advocacy
9 a.m.–6 p.m., Monday to Friday
0300 123 3393
Text: 86463
info@mind.org.uk

Samaritans

Available round the clock to provide confidential support to anyone who needs to talk
24/7, 365 days a year
116 123 (UK)
116 123 (ROI)
jo@samaritans.org

NHS counselling

Information about counselling resources in the UK
www.nhs.uk/conditions/counselling

Campaign Against Living Miserably

Provides an anonymous and confidential mental health helpline and web chat service for men in the UK
5 p.m.–midnight, 365 days a year
0800 58 58 58
thecalmzone.net

B-eat (Beat Eating Disorders)

Supporting anyone affected by eating disorders, anorexia, bulimia, EDNOS or any other difficulties with food, weight and shape
24/7, 365 days a year
0808 801 0677
Youthline: 0808 801 0711
b-eat.co.uk

Bullying resources (UK)

NSPCC

The UK's leading children's charity, preventing abuse and helping those affected to recover
24/7, 365 days a year
0808 800 5000
Childline: 0800 1111
nspcc.org.uk

Bullying UK
Provides help and advice for victims of bullying in schools, work and the community
9 a.m.–9 p.m. Monday–Friday, 10 a.m.–3 p.m. Saturday–Sunday
0808 800 2222

Sexual assault and domestic abuse resources (UK)

National Domestic Violence helpline
A national service for women experiencing domestic violence, their family, friends, colleagues and others calling on their behalf
24/7, 365 days a year
0808 2000 247
helpline@refuge.org.uk

Rape Crisis
Offering support and counselling for those affected by rape and sexual abuse
12 p.m.–2.30 p.m.,
7 p.m.–9.30 p.m.
0808 802 9999
rapecrisis.org.uk

Victim Support helpline
Help and support for anybody affected by a crime
24/7
08 08 16 89 111

Cruelty-free products (UK)

Peta UK's Cruelty-Free Companies search
A directory to look up cruelty-free cosmetics, personal care products and more
http://features.peta.org/ cruelty-free-company-search

Leaping Bunny
Information and shopping guides to help you find certified cruelty-free products
leapingbunny.org

Hello!

Whenever I hear someone say something like,

Change starts with you

or

You are the ruggedly handsome sea captain of your own future

(people definitely do say that), I think to myself that it's all very well *saying* these things, but I can't really imagine how they'll apply to my own life.

Of course thinking positively is helpful. But sweeping generalisations about changing the world or achieving personal happiness simply by thinking, *I will be happy,* aren't quite enough for me. If I'm going to try to reorganise the way my brain thinks, I need to know exactly *what* I'm trying to achieve and precisely *how* it applies to me on a Saturday night when I'm scrolling endlessly through social media and wondering if I should get a drastic hair cut (the answer to that is almost always no).

It's one thing to post inspirational quotes and beautiful bed linen on Instagram to give the impression of a perfect, happy life, and another thing entirely to make actual changes to improve your existence, even if they're not always worthy of the 'gram. Nobody's got their life completely sussed, and anybody who pretends they do is probably an influencer trying to sell you shady 'detox teas'.

Success in life isn't always about making big, dramatic lifestyle changes, overhauling your entire personality or getting rid of all of your personal belongings so that you have room to be the best version of yourself (apparently being in your prime requires a lot of physical space). Instead, it's often little changes we make to how we think – the re-framing of ideas and thought patterns that have been our default for so long – that perk us up and make life a lot more bearable. Dare I say it, even *enjoyable*.

Using positive affirmations (phrases that you repeat to yourself to try to change how you think) is sadly not something I have invented. However, it is something that I hope I can make more realistic and accessible for you. I can't say,

I am the architect of my own destiny

without cringing internally, which somewhat hampers the phrase's ability to change my life and bring me inner peace. However, I can say,

I am building my own future and will do it out of Lego, old Twiglets and Blu-Tack if I have to

because I know that life isn't always a glorious upwards trajectory towards success, but an improvised mishmash of building blocks that help get me to where I want to be.

I doubt you could say,

I love the challenges each day brings!

with a straight face when it's chucking down with rain and your cat's been sick in your shoe, but maybe you'd manage to cling on to,

I can make it through this day and to a bright new dawn tomorrow, hopefully sans cat vomit

because sometimes it's not about trying to be the best you can be – it's just about making it to bedtime without public screaming.

This book is going to cover friendship, romance, mental health and making peace with your body. It's got bits about growing up, navigating education and work, and how to survive social media without giving up and burying your phone at the bottom of a very big hole. Excuse my delusions of grandeur, but it's even got some stuff about how we can all help to make this complicated (and at times headache-inducing) world we're in a slightly better place.

If this sounds like it might be useful to you, then please read on, enjoy and maybe even use a highlighter to pick out some phrases that speak to you. I'm only really suggesting this so that I can feel like I've imparted wisdom as an author. Just do it as a favour to me, so I can die happy. Please?*

*Note to my editor – is it attractive to beg your readers for favours?

Assembling a crack team

To survive in a world that puts you through an emotional spiralizer to create human courgetti, you need to surround yourself with people who love you. Your friends and family are more than just that: sometimes they're your comrades-in-arms, your strangely aggressive backing dancers – and often they're the only ones who can remember where you left your phone.

Despite your crack team, throughout life you'll always come across people trying to mess with your head and ruin your Tuesdays. Love yourself more than anybody hates you. Embrace what makes you different. Wrap yourself up in love like you're a delicious sausage roll, and just hope that nobody eats you.

I am blessed
with family,
friends ...
AND
205
ACQUAINTANCES
ON FACEBOOK

There are times in life when you'll feel utterly friendless. Friendlessness is a sneaky creature, and can strike at any time. It might arrive when you've actually seen friends or family that day, but have no plans for the evening. Suddenly the night stretches ahead of you like a big, yawning motorway and you can't imagine ever being blessed with human company again.

It might also find you when you really haven't been spending a lot of time with other people. Scrolling compulsively through your Facebook feed,

FRIENDLESSNESS IS A SNEAKY CREATURE, **AND CAN STRIKE AT ANY TIME**

you'll feel as if everybody else in the entire world went to a really glamorous-looking music festival in a desert, made friendship bracelets out of their own hair and ate delicious bagels today, without you. Where were your bagels? You deserve bagels. No matter who you are, there are people in your life who care about you and would happily bring you the aforementioned metaphorical or actual bagels.

The Internet has done great things for the world: it has helped to reduce knowledge inequality by trying to make information available to all and has provided us with instant access to videos of premature baby hippos learning to swim. However, it has also made it far easier to compare your Friday night with the Friday nights of celebrity DJs, YouTube millionaires and everybody you went to primary school with.

Karen (who stole your boyfriend back in Year 4 by writing him a particularly witty note while you were meant to be colouring in a picture of a Roman sentinel) is having drinks on a New York rooftop with ten mates, and you're in bed watching reruns of *Friends* with crisp crumbs in your underwear.

A peek inside my brain when I'm feeling friendless would reveal a horrifying scrolling LED display featuring such instant classics as, 'Nobody cares about you, you knob', 'You have no friends and your stories aren't funny', 'You're going to be alone for the rest of your life unless you adopt a snake' and other similar hits. At the time, it doesn't matter in the slightest that none of these things has a basis in fact. At that moment they seem to explain so succinctly why I'm spending the weekend by myself, crying at a really emotional bread advert.

NOBODY CARES ABOUT YOU, **YOU KNOB**

It's worth pointing out that if you have these thoughts a lot, you might be having a rough time with your mental health and I'd definitely recommend seeking some help. There's absolutely nothing shameful, weird or bad about this, and I've included a list of resources at the front of this book for you to take a look at if you do feel you need some support.

It's hard to think logically when you're in a friendlessness spiral, but if you can just hang on to three things, I'd try:

1. Logging yourself out of social media sites for a bit, only keeping the ones that bring you actual joy. After that, Marie Kondo the apps on your phone until all you have left is WhatsApp and a puzzle game that you downloaded in 2014.

2. Focusing on some recent good times you've had with friends or family that might not seem Instagram-worthy but did put a bit of pep in your step nonetheless.

3. Making plans for the future to spend time with your best people, perhaps all lying on your bed together watching *Friends* and videos of premature baby hippos learning to swim, with crisp crumbs in everyone's underwear.

Everybody has different relationships with their friends and family and they're definitely not always sunshine, rainbows and sharing a milkshake with two straws (I assume this is what happy people do – I'm lactose intolerant). But if you have a cousin you can discuss the merits and failings of the Kardashians with, a teammate who lets you eat some of their grapes or maybe a friend willing to text you pictures of their dog when you're feeling sad, then that's a pretty great position to be in.

#HAPPY
#BLESSED

I am there for
my friends
in their hours
of need ...

THROUGH
BREAK-UPS,
DISAPPOINTMENTS
AND REALITY
TV SHOW
CANCELLATIONS

It's easy to be somebody's friend when they're in a great mood, and you're running around laughing merrily and having wild adventures like Thelma and Louise but with slightly-to-entirely less murder. (What? I don't know your life.)

But as people often say when they go through something harrowingly rubbish, you find out who your true friends are when you're really suffering. To be brutally honest, this is because it's often not super fun to hang out with somebody who's sad. Sadness is a bummer, and it's hard to be the life and soul of the party when you're feeling like your heart and stomach have been steamrolled into a grisly organ pancake.

BEING SOMEBODY'S FRIEND ISN'T JUST ABOUT **STEALING CARS AND DRIVING OFF INTO THE SUNSET**

Being somebody's friend isn't just about stealing cars and driving off into the sunset – it's also about being with them when they plummet off the cliff. If you haven't seen *Thelma & Louise* you're probably thinking this is a little bit dark, but I promise it makes sense and I'm not simply pulling weird metaphors out of my odd brain. You don't have to *enjoy* spending time with your friends when they're going through a rough patch – you just have to be there, spending the time.

Different people like to be supported in different ways when it all goes tits up for them (for starters, you probably shouldn't use phrases like 'tits up' when describing their life).

It can be quite difficult to navigate somebody else's feelings, especially if their natural reaction to problems is the total opposite to how you tend to respond. For example, when things go wrong for me I want everybody I know to show up at my flat with crisps and dips, light 200 scented candles, wrap me up in blankets like a human burrito and then feed me the crisps while I cry and make everybody listen to the same sad ABBA song on repeat for hours.

Other people like to be left alone, or to act as if everything's fine, or to only spend time with certain people. This is confusing to me, so I offer the crisps/candle/burrito combo and sometimes feel a bit taken aback when they don't want to be part of my weird sadness ritual. The trick is to work out how you can help somebody in the way *they* need most, rather than the way you imagine they'd like to be helped. This might mean sending supportive texts or funny videos, or checking in with them every day to see how things are going. It might mean bringing them food and helping them out with practical things like cleaning and laundry, or even just spending time with them watching a film in silence. It may not feel like you're actively doing much, but the fact that you're there can sometimes be all that matters.

THE TRICK IS TO WORK OUT HOW YOU CAN HELP SOMEBODY **IN THE WAY** *THEY* **NEED MOST**

Another trap I think we can often fall into is doing something initially to feel like we've supported someone, and then sort of drifting away when they're not instantly fixed. If someone is experiencing problems with their mental health, or bereavement, or any other huge upheaval in their life, it can take quite a while for things to settle down again. Being supportive when something bad first happens is relatively easy. It's how you behave when a friend's heartbreak isn't making headlines in your social circle any more that can really go on to define your friendship.

A person whose self-worth is low because of what's going on in their life might actually ignore or reject your friendship. It's not uncommon, and it can make it pretty tough to stick around and get them through to the other side. Don't start any Taylor Swift-/Katy Perry-level feuds with friends when they're not feeling themselves, and don't take it to heart if your friendship is a little bit one-sided for a while. It won't be forever, and you'll come out of it with a stronger bond than ever.

LIKE TAYLOR SWIFT AND ED SHEERAN.

I must nurture
my relationships
with friends ...

THEY'RE THE
ONLY ONES WHO
CAN DELETE MY
BROWSER HISTORY
FOR ME IF I DIE

When you're a kid, friendship is a very dramatic thing. Friends fall in and out of favour, with regular tears, drama and fisticuffs in the playground. You make friendship bracelets, and only lend your smelly gel pens to your *absolute favourite* people. You buy a 'Best Friends' necklace you can split in half, and swear to wear it until you both die. You announce new relationships with friends to the world, and go

THESE ARE THE RELATIONSHIPS YOU NEED TO NURTURE LIKE LITTLE BABY HEDGEHOGS

through heartbreaking public break-ups because you weren't allowed to play the part of Simon Cowell in your lunchtime game of make-believe *X Factor*.

While it is normal for friendships to fizzle out or come to an end, there are obviously some people that you definitely want to hold on to. You'll have some friends you hope will stick around for life, and eventually attend your wedding/ prime ministerial swearing-in ceremony/funeral (delete as applicable). These are the relationships you need to nurture like little baby hedgehogs.

As an adult, sometimes I'm a bad friend. I often forget to text my friends back for days. I think I haven't seen some mates for a few weeks, and then I check my calendar and find it's actually been a few months. I only know when it's somebody's birthday because Facebook helpfully tells me.

(Although I do always make sure to send them happy birthday messages on every available messaging platform, which must count for something. Ten messages, ten times better friend? Probably.)

When we talk about relationships that need work and commitment, we usually mean romantic ones. Everybody agrees that those sorts of relationships require compromise, attention and sometimes quite a lot of effort to make them run smoothly.

When we mature and reach adulthood (there's no way of saying that without sounding like David Attenborough talking about a species of bird) it's normal to have friends that we don't see every day

MAKE REGULAR PLANS
AND STICK TO THEM

like we did at school or university, or who have moved a bit further away than the house down the road.

We also might focus more on our romantic relationships as they become more serious. This can sometimes make us complacent about maintaining our friendships. Think about it – it would be very odd if you realised you hadn't spoken to someone you were in a relationship with for a week, unless one or both of you were doing some sort of sponsored silence. But when it comes to even my closest friends, I'll be out of touch with them for a while before I see a really good animal video and know I need to send it to the one who's obsessed with watching tiny hamsters eating miniature food on YouTube.

Just because you're not smooching your friends on the mouth (if that's what you're into) doesn't mean that the relationships you hold with them don't need to be worked on and nurtured like a hamster being pampered with a little hamster-sized pancake. If you are used to relatively smooth sailing with your friends, it can be hard to remember that they, just like partners, sometimes want to be told or made to feel that they're loved and appreciated. You might feel weird telling Bob you eat lunch with at work that you love and appreciate him, but maybe you could give him half your sandwich and a handful of grapes. Platonic, reciprocal love grapes.

BE A SHOULDER TO CRY ON, BUT ALSO A SHOULDER TO LAUGH ON UNTIL YOU ALMOST WEE A BIT

Make regular plans with your friends, and stick to them. Notice when someone seems a little down on social media or is sending the group chat slightly sad texts, and make some time to support them and help them get back on their feet. Be a shoulder to cry on, but also a shoulder to laugh on until you almost wee a bit. Ideally not directly on the shoulder.

ALTHOUGH THE PHYSICS OF THAT WOULD BE QUITE IMPRESSIVE.

Every new person
I meet is a
potential friend ...

I WILL APPROACH
THEM WITH DOG-LIKE
ENTHUSIASM, MINUS
THE BUTT-SNIFFING

making new friends is hard. It's a little bit easier when you're in school or university and you're forced to be in close proximity with hundreds or thousands of other people your own age, and you have to ask them things like, 'Please pass the magnesium so I can set fire to it.' But it's not always easy even then, and after you're done with the world of education you

WHERE DO I FIT IN IF THEY'VE ALREADY **FILLED THEIR QUOTA OF HUMAN COMPANY?**

have to put in some real effort to expand your social circle.

We often hear the phrase, 'It's hard to meet people.' If you live in a small countryside village or are currently working on the International Space Station, this is probably true. But if you live in a town or city it's actually quite easy to *meet* people. The difficult part is *connecting* with them. I often look around me and feel like everybody's already made all their friends. Where do I fit in if they've already filled their quota of human company?

The truth is that most people *are* in fact open to making new friends, communicating with strangers and adding a bit of joy to their day in the form of a pleasant interaction (please note, none of this applies on the London Underground). I remember once going to an event where I knew nobody – I got a drink, did a circuit of the room, panicked and then ran out into the hallway to call my sister and complain to her that it was too scary and that I couldn't talk to anybody.

Eventually it was too ridiculous to keep hiding, so I hung up decisively, marched myself back into the room and just ... talked to somebody. Instead of approaching a group who were already mid-conversation (I still haven't worked out how to do this in a way that isn't awkward and don't actually believe it can be done), I saw somebody else on their own, went up to them and asked, 'Are you here by yourself?' She immediately said, 'Yes! Thank god you talked to me, I've just been standing here like a fool!' and I had a friend for the rest of the evening. We even added each other on Facebook.

WE ALMOST ALL FEEL LIKE FOOLS IN NEW SOCIAL SITUATIONS

This was not a great friendship that lasted the test of time, but it meant I had someone to eat free event food with and chat to about how scary the prospect of moving to the city was. Most importantly, it reaffirmed something I had suspected for a long time – we almost all feel like fools in new social situations, and the majority of us would be thrilled to be approached by someone for a chat.

Not every friendship has to involve buying friendship necklaces, making joint Spotify playlists and going on *Sisterhood of the Travelling Pants*-style holidays to Greece. If you enjoy having a good long chat with somebody at your local post office every time you go in to return online shopping, that's a friendship! If you sit next to someone every day and eventually they start sharing their snacks with you, that's *definitely* a friendship (snacks really seal the deal).

If you're struggling to do the actual meeting part of meeting new people, start with joining a club, sports team, society, exercise group or art class relevant to your interests, and then take the next big step: go up to somebody and say hi. If you're feeling bold, you could even say more words after that.

THE WORLD IS YOUR OYSTER.

I am open and honest with the people I love ...

EXCEPT WHEN THEY ASK ME WHAT I THINK OF THEIR BOYFRIENDS

There are certain types of lies that are widely considered to be acceptable. If a pal shows you their new weird *Harry Potter* tattoo, you smile and nod and say it's lovely (I know this, because I have weird *Harry Potter* tattoos and I've never had a bad reaction from one of my friends).

If they want your opinion on somebody they're dating and you secretly think they're nice but a bit dull, you say they're perfect and you're buying a hat (this is baby boomer slang that means you're getting ready for their wedding).

If they ask if you like their new very out-there dress that they've already taken the tags off, with hope shining in their little puppy-dog eyes, you say it's fantastic

IF A PAL SHOWS YOU THEIR NEW WEIRD *HARRY POTTER* TATTOO, **YOU SMILE AND NOD AND SAY IT'S LOVELY**

and cheer them on even if you wouldn't be caught dead in it.

These are known as 'white lies', but I also think they're just an important part of being kind and maintaining relationships. You don't have to tell people every opinion you have about them. If the tattoo is already on their neck, you being honest about hating it and sending them lots of grimacing emojis isn't going to magically leech the ink back out of their skin. Being brutal about their perfectly nice boyfriend or their new dress is going to be very awkward if you *do* end up having to buy a hat to wear while you watch them skip down the registry office hallway in that dress.

There are, however, lies that we get quite used to telling. Lies about ourselves and others that break down our ability to communicate with the people around us. Being honest with a friend about the things in their life that you think are holding them back or that might be unhealthy is extremely difficult. Most people don't like to be told this stuff and might end up getting a bit defensive and retaliate by making fun of your *Harry Potter* tattoos. But ultimately your friends know that you're the person who knows them best, and getting that kind of feedback from you can help give them the perspective they need to make positive changes in their life.

If somebody's got a friend who seems to be really mean to them, telling them you don't think that dynamic is okay might be the first step to them realising this isn't a healthy situation and finding one that actually works for them. If they're terrible with money, flagging it could be the difference between them being able to afford lunch or not that month. These aren't easy conversations to have at all, but sometimes friendship is about telling people the tough things that only a friend could, because nobody else would be close enough to notice or to want to help.

YOUR FRIENDS KNOW THAT **YOU'RE THE PERSON WHO KNOWS THEM BEST**

The other side of this is about being honest with your friends about what you're going through. It's easy to fall into a pattern of telling people we're fine every time we're asked how we are. Sometimes I'll have been openly weeping in the street an hour before someone asks me what's up, and I'll still say, 'Everything's great, thanks!' I do this because it's

BECAUSE I WAS WEEPING ABOUT THE FACT THAT **THERE AREN'T ANY ROYAL PRINCES LEFT TO MARRY**

easier. Because I don't want them to worry. Or maybe because I was weeping about the fact that there aren't any royal princes left to marry any more so I'll always be a commoner – and I don't want them to think I'm weird.

Your friends are the ones who might think you're weird but will love you anyway. Just as you'd want to know what's really going on with them, they want to know what's going on with you. Tell your friends about your victories and your happiest days, but also be open and honest with them if you're feeling like a human slug and need to be carried everywhere today in some sort of adult baby sling.

THEY MIGHT NOT BE ABLE TO CARRY YOU TO WORK, BUT THEY'LL SURE AS HELL TRY.

My company is not a burden ...

HANGING OUT WITH ME MAKES MY FRIENDS AS HAPPY AS THE WOMEN IN YOGHURT ADVERTS

It's Tuesday morning. You text someone asking if they want to hang out with you on Friday. They've read the message and haven't replied. It's now Thursday.

It's a four-sentence horror story if ever I've heard one. I'm really sorry if you're reading this book alone at night and I've scared you. Situations like this are easily navigated by people who feel very sure of themselves and their relationships with friends. If you're one of those people, I salute

THE IDEA OF SENDING A FOLLOW-UP TEXT IN THIS SCENARIO IS **NIGHTMARISH**

you and ask you 'HOW?' But for those of us who often have wobbly moments of insecurity, the idea of sending a follow-up text in this scenario is nightmarish.

It's hard sometimes not to feel like you're bothering people with your friendship. 'If they wanted to hang out with me,' we tell ourselves, impressed at our own owlish wisdom, 'they'd have texted back immediately. In fact, they'd have texted me first.' Having thought about this a lot while agonising over WhatsApp read receipts (it turns out you can turn those off, and I recommend that you do this RIGHT NOW), I've realised that this rationale relies on the idea that I'm the central figure in everybody else's lives. It's like I think I'm the main character in a video game and everybody else only springs to life to ask me for help with their quest when I walk around the corner.

This, of course, is not true. Everybody's living their own messy, complicated lives and I'm just one part of that. A friend not responding to a message or being the first to make plans isn't a sign of a broken friendship or a cue for me to start my life as the local cave hermit/rumoured snake witch. Sometimes

I PROMISE YOU, **YOU'RE NOT A BURDEN TO YOUR FRIENDS**

I'll text first, and sometimes my friends will. Sometimes I'll make the plans, and sometimes I'll wait for people to invite *me* to a water park on a Saturday afternoon (I'm actually still waiting on this one – apparently

adults don't really go to water parks). Sometimes I'll even take days to text back or forget to text back at all.

The issue lies in feeling secure about yourself, and believing that you're worth being friends with – things those aforementioned people who are sure of themselves have mastered. It can be especially tough if you've had bad experiences with friends in the past.

But I promise you, you're not a burden to your friends. They're probably quite fond of you in fact, and won't at all mind if you send a follow-up text, or call them for a chat, or send them a Facebook invite for a group trip to a water park (I'm not letting it go).

As much as you can, try to recognise where those feelings of inadequacy are coming from, realise that they're completely illogical and not actually based on any evidence that your friends think you're a weird shrew person, and then dismiss them. You'll be able to be a better friend to other people when you're being a better friend to yourself.

I know. Deep.

Occasionally, of course, there's someone who really *is* bothering to text you back or make plans with you. In that case, it's not so much you being worthy of their friendship — you have to ask yourself if they're worthy of *yours*.

OH, HOW THE TABLES HAVE TURNED.

I will not rent the spare rooms of my brain to negative people ...

THAT'S WHERE I STORE MY BADMINTON RACQUETS

What is the point of having friends? This is what I've come up with:

So you can spend time with people who share the same interests as you. The Internet has helped people with niche interests – if you're interested in professional *Pokémon* battles, dyeing your hair or a particular breed of lizard, you'll be able to find your people online and talk about those things to your heart's content.

So you can perform the Macarena. It's fine to do it by yourself but it looks a lot grander and more elegant if you do it with others.

To share the highs and lows of your life with your fellow humans – to have shoulders to cry on when your eyes are leaking, and shoulders to sit on when you've won the competitive *Pokémon* championships and need to be hoisted proudly into the air while the crowd cheers you on.

To go on adventures with – whether this involves climbing mountains and camping in forests, or going on madcap jaunts to Sainsbury's wearing animal onesies because you really need salt and vinegar crisps.

What are friends not supposed to do? Your friends are human people just like you and will therefore have flaws and bad times, and that's okay. But they really, *really* shouldn't do any of the below:

Make you feel rubbish about yourself on a regular basis. As we all know, this is why women's magazines and giant billboards featuring airbrushed underwear models were invented. Your friends should never intentionally make you feel bad about how you look, feel, dress or live your life. There's a difference of course between trying to be constructively critical – for example, gently recommending that you shouldn't date somebody who's proven they have the emotional capacity of a slug – and constantly criticising you to bring you down.

Allow you to perform the Macarena by yourself. Ever.

Ditch you when they get a better offer, cancel on you all the time or just generally make you feel like you're their last priority. It's true that sometimes people get busy. I, for example, am ditching all my friends to write this book. But if somebody consistently makes you feel like some sort of understudy friend to be called upon if their main friend is ill, that's no good.

Bring negativity into your life on a regular basis. I'm not going all new-age hippy on you and talking about the *abstract concept* of negative energy. I mean people

who make you feel bad, bring you down, complain constantly or don't let you enjoy the things you like. Sometimes people are negative because they're going through something tough. But sometimes people are just negative. And you don't need that in your life (unless that's what you're into, and really, who am I to judge? That would be very negative of me).

It can be easy to accidentally let people who aren't adding anything nice to your life set up camp in your brain. You should not feel bad about letting them go. You only have so much time and love to give, and you shouldn't be wasting it on people who make you miserable. I'm a fan of the frank and honest conversation about why it's not working. I know it's excruciating, but it's the right thing to do – unless that person is being genuinely abusive and rubbish, in which case you owe them absolutely nothing.

Sometimes it's complicated – if that person is a family member, a teacher, or someone you work or live with, you might not be able to completely exorcise them from your life like a troublesome ghost. All I can recommend is that when they do start getting to you, to go easy on yourself. Try as hard as possible to fill your life and your head with all the delicious joyful things the world has to offer,

SO THAT THE NEGATIVITY HAS TO SHOUT REALLY, REALLY LOUD TO BE HEARD AT ALL.

Let go of the
people who have
let go of you ...

LIKE ROSE AND
JACK ON THE
FLOATING DOOR OF
YOUR FRIENDSHIP

This section is going to be very *Titanic*-heavy, so if somehow you haven't seen *Titanic* (i.e. have been living under an iceberg), I recommend that you watch it before proceeding, or I'll spoil the ending for you and you'll look me up and send me angry messages on Twitter.

The ship is gone. Everybody's trying to stay afloat and wait for rescue. Rose is hanging out on that door, and Jack is having a nice relaxing paddle in the icy water. Rose tells Jack that she'll never let go of him, right? But then Jack sadly perishes. We can argue about whether or not there was room on that door for

ALL IN ALL, IT WOULD HAVE BEEN VERY SAD AND A BIT GROSS

both of them until we're as blue in the face as Dead Jack (sorry, Dead Jack), but people *still* get mad at Rose for letting Jack go.

Let's explore for a moment what would have happened if she *hadn't* let him go. She would have been holding on to her dead boyfriend for ages. It would have made being pulled into a rescue boat very tricky, and slightly awkward for the other passengers. You can imagine one of them politely clearing their throat and saying, 'Ahem – have you noticed that your boyfriend is, in fact, already dead?' Then they would have had to throw him overboard if they needed the space for someone more alive. All in all, it would have been very sad and a bit gross.

Believe it or not, there's a lesson to be learned from this and it's not just that you should never declare your boat to be 'unsinkable' (because we all know how well that ended). Sometimes it really is just time to let go. We like to imagine that our friendships will last forever – sometimes we even buy necklaces that proclaim that to the world. But people change as they grow up or are separated by circumstances or fall out and can't put aside their differences any more. It can be very upsetting when this happens, but it is very normal.

Sometimes friendships might end with a bang, like a turbulent argument about who's the most talented out of Good Charlotte or Avril Lavigne (a real and very intense fight I had with a best friend when I was eleven). Sometimes the other person simply isn't putting enough emotional elbow grease in to be counted as a friend any more. Mostly, friendships just tend to fade out, like a beauty guru's perfect smoky eye-make-up look. It will probably happen to you a few times throughout your life, and it doesn't mean you've failed or that you're bad at friendship. It just means you're moving on to a new phase, and that's okay.

SOMETIMES IT REALLY IS JUST **TIME TO LET GO**

If your friendship does turn out to be dead in the water, the good news is that freeing up the time you've wasted trying to revive it means you can get a small pet, take up calligraphy, make new friends or try your hand at writing an advice book (I hear they're letting anyone do that these days). It can be surprisingly exhausting to give your love and energy to someone and not get any back, or to hold on to something that's a part of who you were rather than who you are now.

Finally letting go, whether that's through having a frank and honest conversation with them about how you feel or by just not bothering to send any more unanswered texts their way, might actually be a bit of a relief.

AND IF YOU ARE LOOKING TO GET A SMALL PET, I'D RECOMMEND A FISH OR A DEGU.

I am not what other people say about me ...

UNLESS THEY'RE SAYING I'M REALLY, REALLY GREAT

Everybody has had awful things said about them. Mother Teresa. The Queen. Probably even David Attenborough, although it's hard to imagine. Here's a short list of things people have said about me:

I'LL DIE ALONE WITH ONLY MY CATS FOR COMPANY.

I'M CROSS-EYED AND I HAVE TERRIBLE TEETH.

I'M NOT FUNNY. I JUST THINK I'M FUNNY, AND IF ANYTHING THAT ONLY MAKES ME EVEN LESS FUNNY.

I DON'T WASH MY CLOTHES PROPERLY (???).

MY BOYFRIEND WHEN I WAS SEVENTEEN DUMPED ME BECAUSE I'M A PRUDE.

I'll admit to the one about not being funny, and statistically I do think it's highly likely that when I move on from this world they'll find my body half-eaten by my cats and/or snakes. But the point is, all of these things were said with a motive – to make me feel bad about myself. We give the things that other people say about us such power, even when it's clear that their goal in saying them isn't to impart some deeply held truth, but to make us sad.

ALL OF THESE THINGS WERE SAID **WITH A MOTIVE**

Sometimes we're affected by these things because we're worried there's a bit of truth in them (what if I *don't* wash

IT'S NOT EASY
TO TAKE THE
HIGH ROAD

my clothes properly? Is there a wrong way to wash clothes?), or sometimes because we just don't like the idea that people think of us in these ways. Mostly it doesn't even matter what's being said – it's the intent to hurt us that stings.

When people are mean about you, it says more about them than it does about you. They're deriving joy from talking rubbish about you in the same way that they probably derived joy from pouring hot water on ants when they were a kid. It's not easy to take the high road. I for one always turn into some sort of medieval knight when insulted, and want to put on chain mail and a codpiece and defend my honour with a duel at dawn. But stooping to the level of bullies is just going to make you feel worse in the long run.

My favourite response to people being awful to me for no reason is to laugh or make self-deprecating jokes and agree with them. I know it's not always easy, but it can be very disarming to somebody who's trying to upset you if you refuse to appear upset. And if their barbed comments aren't hitting the mark, they'll eventually get bored. If somebody is really harassing or bullying you, there's no shame in not being able to laugh that off, and you should talk to somebody about it or report them in an online or offline capacity.

Try not to dwell too much on these things. Accept that they're there and then move on to something positive. For every crap thing somebody says about you, try to remember a good thing that somebody else has said. Really, you don't even have to rely on other people to provide you with reasons why you're great. It might feel self-indulgent, but I'd recommend occasionally writing down a list of all the things that make you somebody you'd definitely want to hang out with. Maybe I don't wash my clothes properly, buddy, but my fashion sense is great.

I'VE GOT A JACKET COLLECTION THAT CHER FROM *CLUELESS* WOULD DIE FOR.

Also … *how does anyone not wash their clothes properly?* I'm kidding, I'm over it, it's fine.

I will not be
part of the cycle
of bullying ...

BECAUSE
THAT'S HOW
SUPER-VILLAINS
ARE MADE

When somebody is rude to you, or goes out of their way to try to intimidate you, or insinuates that your cat isn't cute, it's like they've handed you a burning hot mug of their anger and negativity and said, 'Here, can you hold this for me?' Just like your parents told you when you were eight and somebody had made fun of your choice of gel pen, bullying

I'M SORRY TO PUT THIS ON YOU, BUT **YOU'VE GOT TO TRY TO BE THE BETTER PERSON**

and downright meanness mostly come from people who are feeling bad about something. This isn't an excuse, but it helps to understand where that negativity springs from and how it keeps spreading like a sneeze on an aeroplane.

When somebody hands you their hot, steaming mug of bad feelings, it's tempting to pass it on to the next unfortunate soul who crosses your path, to prevent burnt hands, steamy glasses and the general inconvenience of carrying something around (let me know when I've killed this metaphor and subsequently your interest in this book). But the thing is, taking your anger out on somebody else rarely works.

I'm sorry to put this on you, but you've got to try to be the better person. You've got a few options with the mug.

THAT'S RIGHT, THE METAPHOR PERSEVERES.

You can drink it. You can be like a human shock absorber and accept that somebody's made you feel bad, experience the gross feelings, digest them and (I'm so sorry) pee them out and continue as you were.

IT SEEMS LIKE SUCH AN OBVIOUS THING TO SAY – **HEY, DON'T BE MEAN TO PEOPLE!**

You can wait for the mug to cool down. You can give yourself time to breathe, count to ten before you answer anybody who's annoying you, write a draft of that sassy email and then delete it and write a reasonable version (whatever you do, don't type in their email address until the very end). Eventually your feelings will be as tepid as hour-old tea.

You can put the mug down. You don't have to hold the mug! You didn't even want the mug! Realise that it's not actually necessary to carry it around, and that you do in fact have a choice in the matter.

The alternative is that you keep passing the cup on to the next person and it travels around pissing everybody off and making the world a little bit more negative. That's what starts wars, petty arguments on Twitter and super-villain origin stories (probably). It seems like such an obvious thing to say – hey, don't be mean to people! – but unless you're some kind of perfect dream human, you'll know that it's not always that simple.

To counteract all the bad feelings constantly circulating, try to pass on little chunks of happiness. They'll travel in the same way but instead of creating villains they'll make people connect with each other, save marriages and help more abandoned dogs get adopted (probably). Imagine you're giving someone something magical every time you're kind to them or go out of your way to help them. Let's call it … a flask of joy.

NO? OKAY. FAIR ENOUGH.

I fancy everyone

Is it normal to fancy every single other person who's on the bus with you? Is it fine to fancy nobody? Is it all right to only fancy that one actor from a superhero film with a slightly weird face, and commit to them fully, forsaking all others?

Like, lust and love can be tricky things, but they get a bit less muddled when you realise that whatever you're feeling it really is okay. Whoever you are and whoever you want to smush your face up against, it's all about finding people who make you feel ace, respecting boundaries and making sure yours are respected in return.

It's also about trying as hard as you can not to be so nervous on a scenic first date that you almost throw up on a swan.

Being alone
doesn't mean
being lonely ...
IT MOSTLY
MEANS MORE
CHIPS FOR ME
AND ABSOLUTELY
NO SHARING

Barack and Michelle Obama. Posh and Becks. Minnie and Mickey. All iconic, sexy couples that we're supposed to aspire to be. We're constantly bombarded with imagery of the joys of coupledom. We see them in advertising, the plots of films and books, but also in little everyday ways … Couples holding hands in the street and kissing on the London Underground at 8 a.m. for some reason, pictures on Instagram

NOBODY HAS REALLY GLAMORISED **BEING SINGLE**

of **#LAZYSUNDAYS** spent lounging with other halves or two-month anniversaries celebrated loud and proud on Facebook.

When we think about being single, we think about being 'alone'. Meals for one. Being the seventh wheel when you and all your coupled-up friends go ice skating, and having to hold hands with one of those plastic penguins they use to teach kids how to skate. This is because nobody has really glamorised being single. There aren't that many people writing books and blockbuster films about the joys of independence.

A friend once said to me that when she told colleagues (all around her age and all with partners) that she was going on a date that night, she got responses ranging from an insincere, 'I'm so sad my dating days are long behind me, I'm going to live vicariously through you!' to 'I can't imagine having to date again, I'd be awful at it. I'm so glad I've got Archimedes*!'

*Name has been changed for privacy. Or has it? No, it has.

THIS IS HOGWASH, IF YOU'LL EXCUSE MY FIFTEENTH-CENTURY SWEARING

As you'd expect, these responses did not exactly make her feel great about being single.

Some people have an annoying tendency to think anyone who enjoys being single is 'putting on a brave face', or 'making the best of a bad situation'. This is hogwash, if you'll excuse my fifteenth-century swearing. Being comfortable in your own company and not feeling like you *need* a relationship is one of the greatest skills you can master in life. I take my hat off to anybody who's nailing it.

I like a good relationship as much as the next gal, but there's nothing we're actually missing out on by not having a partner. Friendships certainly aren't any less important just because they're not the romantic kind. There is also a particular kind of comfortable that I think we only feel when we're

BEING TRULY BY YOURSELF MEANS FREEDOM

alone. Even when you're spending time with people you know inside and out, you've got to take a whole other human into account when you say or do things. Being by yourself means true freedom. Freedom to do everything in the exact way that will make you most happy or productive, with no compromise. Whether this means listening to your kind of music, eating your favourite food, going to the places you want to go or maybe just walking around in your pants at home with nobody to observe you.

It seems obvious to say that you can be happy single, but even though we all know this, sometimes we don't fully *know it*. You know? Being single does not represent some sort of failure on our part. There are people who choose never to have a relationship, and that doesn't mean they're missing out on anything in life. They've just chosen a different path to the one sold to us in jewellery ads. When you're alone, you're not missing a half:

YOU'RE JUST YOU, BY YOURSELF, AND THAT'S OKAY.

I will find
the right person
for me ...

AND STOP DATING
PEOPLE WHO
MAKE ME CRY
IN PIZZERIAS

So, you've done it. You've got one of those relationships you've been hearing so much about. You hold hands, skip down tree-lined avenues and share frozen yoghurt on the night bus home while a man next to you vomits into his hat. At some point, everything will stop seeming quite so perfect, but that's normal. You might even realise that you don't quite agree about what your relationship should be. But that's okay, right? If you're willing to compromise on certain aspects of a relationship, then that's fine. Not every difference of opinion means you're doomed to incompatibility.

But I'm here to tell you something I, an adult woman, didn't properly realise until recently: you don't have to compromise on your fundamental needs in a relationship. If there are some things that are vital to you and you're not getting them out of your current situation, you have to weigh up how important they are to you and accept that you might need to have A Serious Talk or possibly even A Sad and Difficult Break-Up.

YOU DESERVE TO BE REALLY, **PROPERLY HAPPY**

Maybe you need more emotional support from a relationship, or more space, or fewer arguments, a bit more fun or somebody who's just nicer to you. If you're not getting it, then don't think it must be your time to settle, or that it's naive to imagine that you could experience something so right and fulfilling. You deserve to be really, properly happy. Every relationship is different – I can't stress that enough –

but they're defined by the people in them and you set your own boundaries for what they involve. If it's not working, and really important bits can't be fixed, you can and should walk away.

It doesn't mean you've failed. It doesn't mean you've wasted your time. It most certainly doesn't mean that you'll never find somebody with the positive qualities that drew you to that person in the first place ever again. Even if your interests are really niche, I promise you there are plenty more people out there with a good sense of humour who also enjoy long walks on the beach, writing *Star Wars* fanfiction and knitting little hats for hamsters (or who will at least be open to trying those things with you).

SOME PEOPLE TRY TO TRICK YOU INTO THINKING THAT **YOU ONLY HAVE ONE SOULMATE**

Some people try to trick you into thinking that you only have one soulmate. That somebody out there is 'the one'. But actually there are probably *thousands* of people you could hang out with/date/smooch that would bring you joy. Somebody might end up being 'the one' because of the meaningful relationship you build together, out of love and trust and having roughly the same idea about what a relationship should be.

Break-ups are tough, you can't get around it, but you don't have to put up with subpar relationships just because you feel emotionally attached to that person. Not to diminish your great and true love for your incompatible partner, but if somebody let you look after their puppy for a few months you'd probably feel about the same amount of distress at the thought of never seeing them again. Does that mean you should be with that puppy forever? Wait … yes, it does! Sorry, I think I've got my analogies mixed up.

Sometimes being attracted to or in love with somebody just isn't enough. If the relationship isn't healthy and it's not making you happy, you need to know that you *can* find one that actually works for you and doesn't end up with you crying hysterically in your favourite pizza restaurant at midnight on your birthday. Not that I'm speaking from personal experience, of course.

BUT COULD YOU PLEASE PASS ME A NAPKIN?

I am sexy and attractive ...

AN ONLINE QUIZ TOLD ME SO

I magine the hottest person you can think of. If it's you, congratulations, you can skip this section because you have achieved body positivity nirvana. If you didn't imagine yourself, take a mental good long look at whoever it was you *did* imagine.

WE *ALL* TEND TO BE VERY CRITICAL OF OURSELVES

Can you picture that person feeling terrible about their face or their body? Can you see them berating themselves for their looks, or feeling inadequate at the gym because they're on the treadmill in between Big Dave and Toned Lara? It seems bizarre but unfortunately we *all* tend to be very critical of ourselves. Even Jason Momoa, who played the very large and muscular (and large) Khal Drogo (did I mention large?)

A LOT ABOUT FEELING ATTRACTIVE **IS RELATED TO CONFIDENCE**

in *Game of Thrones*, has probably looked at himself in the mirror and shrugged morosely. I know. It's hard to believe, but it's true.

A lot about feeling attractive is related to confidence, which can be tricky. Everybody has moments where they feel crap about themselves, but if you can find one good thing that you like about how you're existing in the world today, that's a good place to start. Maybe you're wearing an excellent hat, or you did some exercise today and are high on endorphins.

THERE ARE PEOPLE OUT THERE
WHO PROBABLY FIND SAUCEPANS SEXY

Or maybe you're making an effort to smile at strangers on the train even if they seem unnerved by your positivity and shuffle away from you. Actively reminding yourself of the things you like about yourself is a very good habit to get into.

There are, of course, lots of different ways to be attractive to other people. Your personality, attitude towards others or excellent working knowledge of maritime law can be attractive. Being sexy – if you even want to be sexy – is extremely subjective. There are people out there who probably find saucepans sexy. I'm not saying that you're a saucepan, I'm just saying that regardless of who you are or what you look like, there'll be people very happy to be with you. Don't get too hung up on the saucepan thing.

The serious, hard-hitting truth is that unless you believe in reincarnation, you're only going to be skipping about in the world looking for people to smooch for exactly one human lifetime. Comparing yourself to others or worrying that you're not the poster-person for sexiness is a waste of your precious time and energy.

Acknowledge that you're having those thoughts, think about where they're really coming from – maybe a lack of general confidence is fuelling the fire of sexy doubt – and then wave them away like so many troublesome moths. You are hot as hell. *Especially* when you talk about maritime law.

OOOOH BABY.

I am great just the way I am ...

JUST LIKE MARK DARCY TOLD BRIDGET JONES

For a long time, I thought that it was possible to be a Perfect Girlfriend. I didn't ever actively think these two words, but I was always striving to be a person with a particular set of characteristics that would make me worthy of playing the devil-may-care romantic lead in an indie romcom. These are the characteristics that I thought made you Perfect Girlfriend material:

Being completely fine with never getting a text back – even if I was asking an important and direct question like, 'Do you think David Attenborough watches his own TV shows to soothe himself to sleep?' Also, never sending a follow-up text that was clearly a prompt for attention. The Perfect Girlfriend is far too confident to need validation via text message.

Similarly, being totally chill about how often I got to hang out with who I was dating. If they barely had any time to spend with me or kept flaking on plans, that just demonstrated what a fun, sought-after person they must be! Lucky me, to get to spend time very occasionally with such a gem!

Always looking great, even first thing in the morning, definitely because of my great genes and extremely healthy diet and not because I crept out of bed before the person I was dating and brushed my hair, teeth and eyebrows before they woke up.

Saying the exact right thing at any given moment at the exact right volume, so as to be witty and engaged but not loud or a show-off. Laughing should always be demure and sexy or an adorable giggle, and should NEVER involve accidentally snorting ramen out of your nose because you're laughing so much at your own joke.

Having my own interests and political opinions as long as they didn't clash with my partner's. And if there ever was a clash, de-escalating the discussion accordingly so that I didn't appear to be making a fuss. 'Oh, you don't think sexism is real? Right, yeah, it's a weird one. I guess I don't really agree. Anyway, what should we get for dinner?'

It was basically about being cool, chill, unfussed, unbothered and unfazed by anything and everything. Never making a fuss, being loud or embarrassing or the cause of any conflict — since all of the above could make me more of a liability than an asset.

I GET A BIT TWITCHY IF I'M NOT TEXTED BACK WITHIN FOUR HOURS

As you can probably tell, I thought that being a good partner to somebody, especially as a woman, was all about moulding myself like Play-Doh into what I thought they'd want from me. It wasn't necessarily anything to do with what they actually wanted from me. It was about reducing or removing aspects of my own personality until I could become a minimalist decorative accessory in anybody else's life.

In reality, I get a bit twitchy if I'm not texted back within four hours, and will definitely send follow-up texts that literally say, 'Pay attention to me!' if I'm feeling ignored. I am not chill – I don't think 'chill' has ever been used to describe me – and am terrible at pretending to be so. I laugh like a hyena or Marge Simpson depending on the occasion, and I jump up like a meerkat on guard duty at the mere whiff of an argument about my core beliefs. These things don't make me a bad person to be in a relationship with. They're not necessarily dream traits, but they're who I am.

You shouldn't waste your time trying to be somebody that you're not – it's exhausting. And anyone you truly want to be with will see the 'imperfect' parts of you and be into you anyway (maybe even *because* of those things). Plus, think of all the sleeping time you'd get back if you weren't sneaking out of bed to apply hairspray at 6 a.m.,

JUST IN CASE YOUR PARTNER SAW YOUR NATURALLY FLAT FRINGE AT BREAKFAST AND DUMPED YOU IMMEDIATELY.

I'm an excellent
first date ...

I'D DEFINITELY
WANT TO TAKE
ME HOME TO
MY PARENTS

When I was younger I used to watch TV shows where people seemed really upset if they didn't have a date at the weekend. They'd constantly be trying to get people's numbers, so they wouldn't have to face the thought of being ... *alone* on a Friday night. I thought dating sounded like fun. I was so young and naive back then. When I actually started going out on dates I felt that I had been misled and lied to. I of course immediately resolved to sue all those TV shows for emotional damages.

Dating is basically hanging out one-on-one with someone you often barely know, while simultaneously trying to make a good impression and work out if you can imagine spending a few months watching an entire TV box set with this person (the true test of all relationships). If you love meeting new people and can imagine nothing better than being stuck with a stranger for hours asking them how many brothers and sisters they have or what course they're doing at university, dating is your dream night out. But if you're nervous about it, as many people are, it can feel a bit terrifying and torturous.

You know when people tell you that you should 'just be yourself' on dates? Well, they're wrong. You should definitely be honest about who you are, of course. But there's also nothing wrong with holding back a bit of yourself until you find out more about the person sitting opposite you who's asking you what your first pet's name was and what your favourite subject was at school, like they're trying to guess your Facebook password.

For example, I'm honest about the fact that I'm a slightly unhinged cat person, but I like to hold back on the fact that I carry my cat around like a baby and sometimes pick her nose for her. What? She doesn't have opposable thumbs!

The best thing you can do when it comes to dating is decide to have fun. At the end of the day you're just two people who are both probably quite nervous, both trying to be open to the idea of love or lust or a bit of company, and both probably about ten per cent more sweaty than you'd usually be if you were hanging out with a friend. I actually like to pretend I'm meeting up with a new friend when I'm going on a date, because it takes some of the pressure off. And there really is no pressure for it to be anything more. If you decide you're not into this person, you can just have a pleasant evening discovering interesting facts about somebody new. Like a platonic rock collection of personality traits (I hope all rock collections are platonic but I'm not here to judge).

THE BEST THING YOU CAN DO WHEN IT COMES TO DATING IS DECIDE **TO HAVE FUN**

You should never feel pressured to kiss someone (or do anything else for that matter) on a date. I know that even if that particular person doesn't seem to be pressuring you it can sometimes feel like every romantic comedy you've ever watched is doing it on their behalf. But it is very much okay to hug, handshake or awkward-wave your date goodbye. I went on a date with somebody at university who lived one street over from me. I had decided about twenty minutes into our date that I wasn't really feeling it. He walked me home, and was going to continue past his street and take me all the way to my front door. In a moment of sheer panic based on the notion that he might want to kiss me when we got to my house, I said, 'I'm all right from here, farewell!' followed by a sort of eighteenth-century bow, and legged it.

I still got a text saying he'd had a nice time and would like to do it again, so apparently even exiting like I was a minor character in a Shakespearian farce didn't ruin his evening. And if I can be a good date, you can too. Go forth and meet new people, enjoy yourself, take the pressure off – and wipe your sweaty hands on your coat before you greet your date.

NOBODY EVER NEEDS TO KNOW.

I'm much more than my relationship ...

I AM ALSO AN AXE-THROWING ENTHUSIAST

Isn't it cute when couples finish each other's sentences? I haven't done a proper survey on this, but my guess is that 100 per cent of people would say, 'Absolutely not, and anybody who does this will be instantly blacklisted from all my future group chats and Halloween parties.' But when you spend a lot of time with somebody, like you tend to do in relationships, your brains begin to merge a bit. Your speech patterns become similar and you might start saying the exact same thing at the exact same time, while your friends all roll their eyes and pretend to vomit.

SOMETIMES IT FEELS LIKE YOU'VE MORPHED INTO **SOME KIND OF TWO-HEADED FRANKENSTEIN'S MONSTER**

That closeness can be lovely, but sometimes it feels like you've morphed into some kind of two-headed Frankenstein's monster with bits of you and your partner all mushed together to form one full entity. Especially if people start referring to you just as 'SarahandRebecca', or maybe even if things are really bad, 'Sabecca'.

Holding on to a sense of your own individual identity is important, not least because relationships don't always last forever and it can make life a lot harder if you've given up things you care about and enjoy to give your relationship top billing at all times. It's true that relationships can take up a big chunk of your time, but make sure you still reserve evenings to enjoy your favourite hobbies, watch your guilty pleasure TV shows, eat the food your partner thinks is gross and even just spend some quality time with yourself. If the person you're in a relationship with wants to get involved with the things you love, that's great! But that doesn't negate the need for 'me time', a phrase so awful that I immediately regret typing it.

'ME TIME', A PHRASE SO AWFUL THAT I IMMEDIATELY REGRET TYPING IT

Making time to see your friends and family, especially without bringing your partner along as a perpetual plus-one, is often one of the things that can suffer. I'm sure your best friend loves your boyfriend dearly, but that doesn't mean they want to see him as much as they want to see you. Some people seem to become completely incapable of socialising solo once they're in a serious relationship, and that can often drive wedges between friends, who start to feel like they've lost their mate to the aforementioned Frankenstein's flesh quilt you've become.

If you find that you're always the one in your relationship who has to compromise or give up time for the things or people you love, you may have accidentally fallen into the availability trap. Victims of this are people who will always rejig their week to make room for their relationship, because that relationship is top priority, meaning their axe-throwing lessons have to take a back seat. It might be that your partner doesn't even realise how much you're giving up in order to focus on them. If you're always willing to change your plans and run your life around theirs, they'll just think it's normal that you're always available when they need you or that you love their hobbies and friends so much that yours aren't so important any more.

Don't let your relationship absorb you into it like some kind of horrifying sci-fi monster that leaves your friends wondering if you still exist. Talk to your partner about the fact that you need time to do the things that make you the person they're super into.

AND HAVE A LITTLE TALK WITH YOURSELF ABOUT WHAT YOU WANT TO PRIORITISE TOO.

I deserve
a great love ...

BUT IT DOESN'T
HAVE TO BE
#COUPLEGOALS

o you ever feel like everybody else somehow seems so much more in love than you are? You might be perfectly happy with your relationship, but it's normal to compare it to the relationships you see around you – especially on social media. After all, is your relationship even worth having if it isn't **#COUPLEGOALS**? Here are some things that are apparently **#GOALS**-worthy:

Going running together first thing in the morning, sporting matching sweatbands and perky 7 a.m. smiles. It doesn't matter if you only managed to run for twenty minutes because you kept fighting about one person going too fast and leaving the other behind, or that you were then both late for the rest of your day. Smile for the picture!

Sharing perfect memories in front of the Eiffel Tower/ Leaning Tower of Pisa/Tower of London/other towers and monuments from your worldly and romantic travels together early on in your relationship. With the right filter, nobody can tell that you're sunburnt, grumpy and extremely disillusioned from having to share a bathroom properly for the first time and fully experience each other's bodily functions.

Glamorous date nights out, where you both dress up and provocatively feed each other chips. It doesn't matter that

this has bankrupted you for the month and you'll be eating distinctly non-fancy beans on toast in your pyjamas for the foreseeable future. The people of Facebook will never know.

Buying each other extravagant gifts for Christmas, so you can both post glossy pictures of watches and tech in front of the tree with #boydonegood, #girldonegood or whatever applies, and then spend an hour editing the pictures, posting them and then reading and replying to the comments instead of making eye contact with each other on Christmas morning.

Spending Friday nights in together on the sofa instead of going out with friends, proclaiming on social media that you'd much rather do this anyway. Proceeding to watch inane TV and stare at each other until you're convinced you'd rather stick a fork in your eye than spend another second on this sofa.

As you may have gathered, my point here is that taking well-framed Instagram pictures together to give the impression that your relationship is a perfect dream, doesn't mean that you're actually *living* that dream. People like to present their best selves on social media, of course, and especially when it comes to love they often want to shout about how well things are going. But to compare yourself to the social media 'ideal' or expect that of your actual relationship isn't healthy.

I'm not saying that people who post the sort of pictures I've described aren't happy – I'm sure lots of them are. But you don't need to be picture-perfect on social media to have a great relationship. The pressure to do that might actually be a bit detrimental to you and your partner. Many people,

YOU DON'T NEED TO BE PICTURE-PERFECT ON SOCIAL MEDIA TO HAVE A GREAT RELATIONSHIP

throughout history, have had great relationships – before social media was even invented (I know, I'm as surprised as you!). If they wanted to impress, they had to commission a portrait of themselves eating avocado on toast in bed with their pugs scattered around them. Best to enjoy the imperfect moments, take pictures when the moment strikes you and never, ever use the hashtag:

#COUPLEGOALS

I belong only
to myself ...

MIND, BODY,
EYEBROWS –
THE WHOLE
PACKAGE

I 'm going to talk about consent for a moment. If that's something you might find tricky to read for your own personal reasons then I won't be at all offended if you skip to the next section or put this book down for a while and go and watch videos of dogs playing with dolphins. They're really very good.

WE HAVE AGENCY OVER OUR OWN BODIES

I want to start with the fact that I strongly believe we aren't being educated enough about sexual consent. It should be mandatory for us to learn as kids that our bodies belong to us, and nobody else is ever entitled to them. We should be taught that consent is enthusiastic, and not just the absence of

WE SHOULD BE TAUGHT THAT **CONSENT IS ENTHUSIASTIC**

'no', as well as the fact that we *can* say no. We shouldn't make kids hug people, even their relatives, if they don't want to. We need to know from an early age that we have agency over our own bodies.

It's not consent if you freeze up and don't reciprocate, if you're being coerced or forced, if you're wasted or asleep, if you've done sex-related things with this person in the past, if you're wearing a short skirt or even if you're completely nude. It's not consent if the other person is in a clear position of power and is abusing that position.

You should never feel guilty or at fault if you have been coerced, assaulted or abused. I know we often have a tendency to think, *I should have done things differently* ... but please don't. Thousands of years of social conditioning have taught certain people, mostly women, that we should keep quiet rather than embarrass, cause a scene or possibly risk violent retaliation. It has also taught other people, mostly men, that a 'no' can turn into a 'yes' if they're persistent enough. This is not okay.

PHYSICAL ABUSE COMES IN MANY FORMS AND CAN SOMETIMES **ESCALATE QUICKLY**

Of course, abuse isn't just sexual. Physical abuse comes in many forms and can sometimes escalate quickly. Emotional abuse can involve your partner being outright threatening or controlling, insulting or undermining you, conditioning you to feel bad about yourself so that you come to rely on them and feel you can't leave.

If any of this sounds familiar to you, please speak to somebody – a friend, a relative, a therapist, anyone you feel you can trust. I am not qualified to help, but there are many people who are, and there is a list of resources in the front of this book if you want to speak anonymously to someone who's waiting for your call.

The tide has been turning lately when it comes to people taking all types of harassment, assault and abuse seriously. It has been a long time coming, and we're still not there yet, but with big movements to hold people accountable for their actions and support for people coming forward with stories, we are making some progress.

I want you to know that if anything like this has happened to you there will be people who believe you, and support you, and who love you and will try to help you work through this. For every sceptic, there are hundreds of people who will have your back. There are professional resources available to you, there are legal routes in place if that's the way you want to go, but also there is no pressure for you to respond in any particular way.

THERE WILL BE PEOPLE WHO BELIEVE YOU, AND SUPPORT YOU, AND WHO LOVE YOU

Nobody is entitled to you, nobody should have control over you, and anybody who wants those things from you is wrong.

FULL STOP.

I am secure in myself and my relationship ...

AND WILL NOT BE JEALOUS OF ANYONE, NOT EVEN BEYONCÉ

For those of you who have never experienced real romantic jealousy, it might seem like a trifling thing often employed by soap-opera writers to inject a bit of drama into yet another episode where someone fakes their own death or another pub burns down. Maybe you've experienced little pangs of jealousy in the past, but have been able to squash them quickly down and continue with life as normal.

THE PROPER, BURNING, ILLOGICAL JEALOUSY THAT CAN DO REAL DAMAGE

This bit of the book isn't about that. It's about the proper, burning, illogical jealousy that can do real damage to relationships (and friendships). I have experienced it, and I know how awful it is from both sides. First of all, if you or your partner are experiencing jealousy and it has led to attempts to control the other's life, their contact with friends or anyone they might be attracted to, this is not okay – and might be emotional abuse. Please do speak to somebody you trust if this sounds all too familiar.

Jealousy might be triggered by an experience in the past where somebody broke your trust, which has made it hard for you to trust again, like the brooding love interest in a romance novel. Sometimes it may seem to have come from nowhere. Either way, it's about feeling insecure. When you're secure, you're not worried about the time your partner spends with others, or upset if you feel like they're paying somebody else more attention than you. When you're happy in yourself and in your relationship, you're not expecting disaster at every turn, convinced that any moment Beyoncé will come and steal your partner away from you.

Insecurity might come from the fact that you feel neglected or let down by your relationship, or it might come from doubt about yourself. After all, if you're not feeling great about yourself, why would you expect somebody else to? Either way, it rarely seems to come from logical fear that a partner is going to leave you and run off with their best friend, with you becoming the tragic side character in a noughties romcom.

You might have very real issues to address with your partner, and those should be explored. But if it all seems to be coming from your own meddling brain, it might be

KEEP CALM AND CARRY ON, AS TERRIBLE UNION JACK CROSS-STITCHED PILLOWS ALWAYS ADVISE

more about working out how you can cope with and move past these feelings. Figure out what you're actually insecure about and see if you can talk it through with someone who will listen and understand. Discuss your feelings with your partner and acknowledge where they're really coming from, rather than have an argument in the heat of the moment about something that you know is illogical.

I'll tell you the magical secret of how I got over my feelings of insecurity and jealousy – first of all, I got lots and lots of therapy, and the importance of this can't be overstated. Second of all, I decided to employ the old 'fake it until you make it' trick. This works in lots of scenarios. I would acknowledge that I was illogically upset, but decide to proceed as if I weren't, and eventually I'd stop feeling upset. I learned how to talk myself down, how to take a deep breath and then keep calm and carry on, as terrible Union Jack cross-stitched pillows always advise.

Some books and films will try to tell you that jealousy is a normal part of a relationship, or that it's even romantic: Edward is so very jealous of Bella hanging out with that dog-man in *Twilight*, and it makes him smoulder *ever so much* – but it's not romantic. Feeling secure and happy within yourself and your relationship is pretty darn romantic if you ask me.

I DON'T KNOW WHY I SUDDENLY SOUND LIKE SOMEONE'S DAD OR A JOLLY LOCAL VICAR, AND I APOLOGISE.

My break-up
will not
break me ...

AND IF IT DOES,
I WILL PUT
MYSELF BACK
TOGETHER LIKE
HUMAN LEGO

anguish and forty per cent regular human person one day, but then accidentally look at their Twitter account and jump back up to seventy per cent anguish for a while. But you'll reach a moment where you realise it's fifty-fifty, and then thirty-seventy, and for a long time it might stick around at a solid ten per cent. A little pang of pain will pop up every time you hear the song you danced to that one time that they probably don't even remember. But ten per cent isn't so terrible any more, is it? It's most definitely survivable.

As you may have noticed, I've tricked you into listening to me say *time heals all wounds*. Sorry, but it's an irritating saying for a reason. Focusing on your friends and family and letting them know that you need them right now can also help heal all wounds. As can indulging your own interests, especially ones that were entirely separate from your relationship. Always remember to rejoice in the little happy moments you have during your grieving process. It doesn't matter if they're fleeting, they are still proof that even in the depths of your sadness well, you can still see a little sliver of light at the top,

AND IT REALLY IS WORTH REACHING.

Making friends with your body

You only get one body, unless you're a surprisingly adept, born-after-your-time grave robber. It's easy to fall into the trap of spending far too much of your time at war with it. Lay down the tabloid photos of celebrity imperfections, those terrifying magnifying mirrors that make your face look like new exclusive satellite images of Mars, or the box of tampons that tries to tell you periods are your little secret.

Make peace with your body. Be nice to it. Read it little poems. Train it to be great at naps, or break dancing, or axe-throwing. Take it on field trips to the countryside, and don't be too hard on it if it doesn't always do exactly what you want it to. You're on the same team.

I am more than
how I look ...

IF THE WIND
IS RIGHT,
I CAN ALMOST
JUGGLE

The world puts a lot of emphasis on how we look. There is no avoiding this. I have tried, but I was told that I can't wear a white bed sheet with round eye-holes cut into it in my day-to-day life. It's far too spooky and nobody wants to be friends with a very average-looking ghost. Even in the ghost world, beauty standards are high.

EVEN IN THE GHOST WORLD, **BEAUTY STANDARDS ARE HIGH**

It's impossible to talk about beauty standards and what's considered attractive without taking into account all the social systems at work that determine what we consider to be 'hot'. The ideal tends to vary between different countries and cultures. The predominant ideas about beauty where I'm from often shut out people who aren't slim, white, cisgender and able-bodied. As a person who benefits from a lot of the structures put in place to shut other people out, I can't speak to the experiences of those people, so I recommend that you seek out different perspectives.

Instead, I can only speak to you from my perspective, and hope that some of it rings true with you too. I have spent a lot of time trying to look certain ways, be a certain weight, dress to look more like I have my life together, and obtain the glossy hair of an expensive racehorse. How I feel when I navigate the world is very strongly tied to how I look, and I think it's the same way for a lot of people. Unlearning that feeling, although tough, is definitely worth attempting.

When someone first meets you, it's true that your appearance might factor into their first impression of you. It might be front and centre if you've done something particularly striking with how you look on that occasion – impersonating Cher or wearing a hot dog costume, for example. But for the most part, once they start getting to know you, your physical appearance is extremely low on their priority list. When deciding whether or not they want to befriend/marry/form a quiz team with you, there are a lot of things that are *far* more important.

I'M NOT SAYING WE SHOULD ALL BECOME PERFECT, SELFLESS ANGELS WHO ONLY DRESS IN OUTFITS MADE OF RECYCLED PILLOW CASES

Think about it. Do you ever consider how your friends look when you're trying to work out who to invite to your birthday party, or who would be the bridesmaids at your imaginary wedding? Or do you think about who's the kindest, most supportive, understanding or trusted? Are you more likely to hang out with somebody because they have a better wardrobe, or because they make you laugh or always pick up the phone when you need them?

There is nothing wrong with wanting to look good, or with celebrating when you do feel great about the face you're presenting to the world. If those things do it for you, more power to you. And I'm not saying we should all become perfect, selfless angels who only dress in outfits made of recycled pillow cases because our inner selves are all that matter. But our inner selves *do* matter more than we consider on a day-to-day basis.

When you're on your deathbed, or your death horse, or however you plan to die, there is no way you're going to be thinking fondly about your favourite outfits or the summer you took up golf and got really toned in very specific places (I've been told golf is a sport so I assume that at least one part of you must get ripped. Maybe the wrists?). You'll be thinking about whether or not you added value to the world, were a good friend or family member, or made a difference with the time you had.

The good news is that all of these things can be achieved without the perfect fishtail braid and/or chunky abs

THAT LOOK LIKE THEY'VE BEEN CREATED WITH A WAFFLE IRON.

My body is
capable of great
things ...

AND SOME PRETTY
WEIRD THINGS,
BUT LET'S FOCUS
ON THE GREAT

Talking about bodies is weird, because everybody has a different experience of living inside their earthly flesh cage (gross), so there aren't entirely universal truths that can be applied to everyone. For example, I want to talk about all the incredible things our bodies are capable of doing, but I can't do that without taking into account the fact that different bodies have different abilities. Some people with disabilities or chronic illnesses, for example, might read the title of this section and think, 'That's easy for you to say, you nincompoop,' and that would be an entirely fair judgement.

It's incredible that we were even born, that we exist at all on this planet. The likelihood of you being the person you are, and existing in the world, is very slim, so it's pretty cool that you're here. I apologise if anybody is reading this from *in utero*

EVERYBODY HAS A DIFFERENT EXPERIENCE OF LIVING INSIDE THEIR EARTHLY FLESH CAGE

and is furious that I'm assuming you're in the outside world rather than the womb. From the point of being born onwards, there are varying levels of things that our bodies are capable of, but hopefully the things over the page will be possible for you and seem as amazing to you as they do to me.

Sleep

Sleep is probably one of my all-time favourite activities. It's a miracle, and I'm so glad we're allowed to do it. Thank you, evolution. Did we evolve to be able to sleep? Surely sleep had to be built in from day one, or did we just crack on with things until we were so exhausted our brains shut off? Impossible to tell as I refuse to do any proper research on the matter. Anyway, back to the point – sleep is amazing. Our bodies and minds mostly switch off for a while so that we can rest, recharge and have disconcerting dreams in which we accidentally cheat on our partners with a member of One Direction who we've never found attractive while awake.

Learning

Our bodies are also capable of learning new skills, and somehow can do certain things automatically with minimal supervision once we've learned them. Have you ever tried to do some physical action, with no active thoughts about how you're going to do it, only to find that your hands remember, even if you don't? I'm terrible at the piano, but I can still play simple pieces that I learned when I was nine and refused to practise because all I wanted to do was trade *Harry Potter* cards and send flirty notes to Ethan, my Year 4 boyfriend. I couldn't tell you where the letters sit on a computer keyboard, but I just typed this sentence with my eyes shut to see if that matters – and it doesn't! Somehow my hands and some secret part of my brain are working together so that I don't have to think too hard about typing. Thanks, team.

Sensory feelings

The fact that we can feel things, not emotions (although those too) but actually touch things with our hands and experience how they feel is incredible. I know I'm starting to sound like a corny yoga teacher, but just being able to experience textures — the feeling of sun on our skin, holding somebody else's hand — they all really knock it out of the park. Have you ever touched an incredibly soft cat or a perfectly bumpy wall? Would recommend.

Laughing and crying

Laughing makes no sense and I love it. Natural endorphins that come from little chuckles and smiles, or from that kind of infectious giggling you do where by the end of it you feel a bit sick, your mouth hurts and you half hope that you never laugh again. On the flip side you have crying, which is cool as well: letting your feelings out in a way that makes them exist physically can be so cathartic, even if you do end up with tiny eyes like shrivelled old raisins.

Our bodies might not always do exactly what we want them to, but there's a whole lot of cool junk going on under your skin and sometimes it feels nice to appreciate the little things. The world's not always a fun or fair place, so we'll take the positives where we can get them! Thanks, body.

PLEASE STOP MAKING ME NEED TO FART DURING PILATES.

I look great today ...

EVEN IN A FRONT-FACING PHONE CAMERA OR FROM BELOW

Feeling good about how you look can sometimes feel like an endless battle. I often wonder if other animals have the same issues we do when it comes to making peace with their faces and bodies. There are lots of different species who try to improve or use their outward appearance to find mates, but when a fish is flashing its special sexy scales or a bird is doing a jazzy mating dance, I doubt that they agonise over any perceived mistake and then go home and mope over a bucket of Häagen-Dazs because they're worried they made a tit of themselves (PLEASE NOTE my excellent bird pun).

OBVIOUSLY LOOKING GOOD **IS COMPLETELY SUBJECTIVE**

Obviously looking good is completely subjective, and nobody's ever going to agree on exactly what it entails. There are people who comment on photos of supermodels to say that they think their hands are weird or they look like they're mid-sneeze. I know this because I just went on a supermodel's Instagram to see what the general public thought of their latest selfie. If people can find flaws in supermodels – people who are PAID to look great – then I am quite sure they would not give me kind reviews.

FOUR OUT OF TEN. VERY UNEVEN FINGERNAILS. TOO MANY BREADCRUMBS IN HAIR.

As hard as it is to tune out unhelpful thoughts such as comparing yourself to others or rating yourself out of ten (as I have just demonstrated by doing both), it's worth trying to reframe the attitude you have towards your appearance by working out what makes you *feel good* first, and then everything else second.

I CAN SPRAY SOMETHING IN MY HAIR, BRUSH IT, AND THEN COAST FOR A WHILE ON THE NATURAL HIGH OF SOFT BEACHY WAVES

When I'm trying to think positively about how I look, I like to focus on the things I actually have a say in on a regular basis – for example, clothes and make-up, rather than my face and body. Nobody gets to make a daily choice about how they're fundamentally structured, but they do get to choose a hairstyle, a comfy jumper or maybe a jaunty beret. For that reason, I also only tend to compliment people on the things they've chosen for themselves.

For me, thinking, *I look great today* has to be grounded in the little things. I can't change my whole perception of beauty in the fifteen minutes I allocate to making myself look nice at the beginning of the day, but I can spray something in my hair, brush it, and then coast for a while on the natural high of soft beachy waves.

It's impossible to ignore the fact that different cultures and societies have beauty standards and ideals that we all feel pressure to live up to. I'm not going to pretend that I, a privileged white woman with a book deal, can solve the problem of feeling good about how you look on a day-to-day basis with a few paragraphs, or even begin to address the complexities it presents. But I hope you can reach for some of the thoughts above when you're feeling down because

YOU'VE ACCIDENTALLY SEEN YOURSELF IN YOUR PHONE'S FRONT-FACING CAMERA.

Nobody else is paying attention to my flaws ...

THERE'S TOO MUCH INTERESTING STUFF ON NETFLIX

There's a lot of cool stuff to look at in this world. We've got the sky, trees, passing wildlife, people wearing fancy scarves driving those weird old-fashioned cars to motor rallies at the weekend. When you think about it, the idea that the people around us are focusing on our physical flaws, out of all the things around them they could be paying attention to, is a bit ridiculous.

I don't mean to diminish how you feel about any flaws that you might perceive yourself to have. I know how much stuff like that can get into your head and dominate your inner monologue. I once over-plucked my eyebrow and it took days for my dented self-esteem to recover. Plus I looked really startled at very ordinary things people were saying to me. The man at the Co-op must have thought I was HORRIFIED at the price of olives.

WHAT EVEN COUNTS AS A 'FLAW', ANYWAY?

Seriously though, if I'd asked that man what he thought of my eyebrows, he probably would have said, 'Fine. Next customer, please. *Please.* I don't want this customer any more.' The things that we think are glaringly obvious to everybody else aren't even blips on their radar. Not to be rude, but people just aren't that interested in looking at your face. Even the people who *love* to look at your face – maybe your parents, best friends or a romantic partner who's really into staring – probably don't notice the things you do. And even if they do, they're not going to mind. That's the beauty of tricking somebody into caring about you (kidding). Your physical appearance is a tiny, inconsequential part of why they like you!

What even counts as a 'flaw', anyway? If we're all agreed (and I hope we are) that societal beauty standards are rubbish and not how we should determine our worth, why is any deviation from them still deemed a flaw? Rejecting beauty norms is one of those things that is easy to preach about but really tough to internalise. Graduating from thinking of your 'flaws' as just differences from the 'ideal', and then eventually managing to be chill with the things you used to agonise over (or even celebrate them) can be a long road.

One of the things that I've suffered with for a long time and have always been hyper-conscious of is having spots and acne. I've had spots since I was twelve and they don't seem to be going away just because I'm now old enough to rent a car in every country. Something like this can really chip away at your confidence. I always imagine that when my skin is bad, even if I've smothered it in a thick layer of make-up to try to disguise my actual face, people are looking at me and making judgements about me. Maybe they think I'm gross! Maybe they think I'm dirty!

Or maybe, just maybe, it doesn't matter. When we're not looking at celebrities who have been so airbrushed that they look like terrifying CGI people, we actually find that we're looking at *normal* people who aren't shiny and perfect. When I pop to the shops with no make-up on, with my real human skin exposed to the world, people don't shrink away in horror and duck behind the till to get away from me. It's worth noting that anybody who would do this because of a physical difference you might have wouldn't be worth impressing anyway.

Those things you're hung up on, you're not going to feel okay about them overnight, but please know that other people really aren't paying as much attention to them as you are. They've got more important things to focus on, and — let's be honest —

SO DO YOU.

I will put
feeling good
first ...

AND FEELING
SMUG FIFTH –
NOBODY'S PERFECT

There is no perfect way to live your life. This fact is not very profitable for companies that sell juicers and personal training sessions with very sculpted men called James. But it's true. The narrative that we're all striving to be super-fit, kale-munching yoga fiends with perfect posture is so prevalent that it's easy to get caught up in it and not think about what you actually want for yourself and your life.

Is it really that important *to you* to be

SPENDING YEARS OF YOUR LIFE TRYING TO FORCE YOURSELF TO DO SOMETHING YOU DON'T EVEN ENJOY THAT MUCH **MIGHT NOT BE WORTH IT**

ridiculously physically fit? There are of course benefits to doing exercise, both mental and physical, but it's genuinely not for everybody. Spending years of your life trying to force yourself to do something you don't even enjoy that much might not be worth it. If you're able to, things like going for a nice countryside walk, frolicking with the lambs in the springtime or swimming outdoors when it's really hot are lovely additions to life. But trying to become a runner, a weightlifter or a basketball champion when you don't like doing those things isn't a necessary part of life.

There are certain ways of exercising that I enjoy, and some that I absolutely hate. The kind I like – swimming in the sea, long hikes in beautiful scenery, obscure dance workout classes – won't ever turn me into a rippling, muscled Adonis. But that's okay! Because that's not an important priority for me. I have higher priorities, like sorting all the different ways you can eat potatoes into a ranked list, and trying to get my cat to wear a bow tie.

Food is also a complicated issue that often seems to involve a lot of restrictions and rules that don't necessarily make us very happy. I can't stress enough that I'm really not a qualified therapist, so if you have issues with food that are affecting your quality of life, I'd recommend that you stop reading this section ASAP and speak to somebody who knows more about it than I do.

I HAVE HIGHER PRIORITIES, LIKE SORTING ALL THE DIFFERENT WAYS YOU CAN EAT POTATOES INTO A RANKED LIST

There's been a 'clean eating' fad going on for a while now that advocates the idea of some foods being 'bad' and others 'good', some 'clean' and others 'unclean' – and honestly, it's nonsense. Balance is good. If you're not keen on eating animals or animal products, cool. But restricting yourself in a way that makes you unhappy? Not cool. No food is 'clean' or 'unclean'. Everything in the world is made up of chemicals. A juice cleanse isn't going to get rid of your 'toxins', it's just going to help you do poos with the consistency of old Cup-a-Soup. I know some people eat purely because their body requires energy to keep going, and that's a perfectly sensible reason to eat food. But food can also be a joyful, nourishing thing.

FOOD CAN ALSO BE **A JOYFUL, NOURISHING THING**

My point is this — what you do with your body when it comes to health and fitness is totally up to you, and just because lots of celebrity influencers on Instagram all seem to be striving for exactly the same body and diet, doesn't mean that's what's going to make you happy. I'm not saying that nobody wants to be a total gym bunny who enjoys the natural high of working out and digs the taste of wheatgrass — if it brings you joy, follow your heart! But however you choose to live, try putting feeling good first before anything else,

AND WORK OUT EXACTLY WHAT THAT MEANS FOR YOU.

I will become one with the great outdoors ...

OR AT LEAST WITH THE PARK ROUND THE CORNER FROM MY HOUSE

As we approach a dystopian future where all jobs, partners and pets have been replaced with supercomputers, we're spending a lot of time looking at screens and monitors. Many people have jobs which require eight hours a day of gazing at a painfully slow desktop, then take fun breaks to look at social media on their phone, followed by going home to watch TV or Netflix or videos of people creating real miniature food on YouTube. It's a lot of screen time.

I enjoy looking at the little glowing cubes as much as the next girl, but I also firmly believe in the mystical healing power of the outside world. I don't know what the science behind it is, but being able to see the sky, some birds, and maybe even be in the vicinity of a tree can be incredibly refreshing.

I'm not saying you have to become an ardent hiker, with proper walking boots and those little ski poles for climbing hills and whacking stinging nettles out the way, or suddenly become a Person Who Camps. I love the outdoors and I still think that camping is more like a punishment than a holiday.

I STILL THINK THAT CAMPING IS MORE LIKE **A PUNISHMENT THAN A HOLIDAY**

Regardless of where I go or how many wet wipes I take with me, I always look like something truly harrowing has happened by the time I get home. And there's always, *always* a glob of mud in at least one of my eyebrows.

Embracing the great outdoors might just mean going for little walks on your lunch break. Even if you live in the middle of a city, there's probably a lone tree standing somewhere that you can visit, or some nice weeds growing up through a pavement. Why not take things a step further and visit a local park? In the summer, parks are the ideal place for a wholesome picnic with your friends, and in the winter, you get to stomp around for a bit and 'get the blood pumping' as old people often say, and then retreat back into the warmth feeling like you've truly earned a cup of tea.

I ALSO NEED TO BE WITHIN TEN MILES OF A NANDO'S OR I THINK MY BODY WILL CRUMPLE

You might even fancy venturing into the countryside. I love the countryside immensely, right up to but not including the point of wanting to live there. I love the peace and quiet, the plants, the wildlife. However, I also need to be within ten miles of a Nando's or I think my body will crumple in on itself like a tin can in space. If you're from a city, like me, the countryside offers something we're not really used to – fresh air! It's funny and slightly terrifying how much of a difference you notice when you're not breathing in toxic car pollution, but instead just the gentle fumes from fermenting cow pats.

If you've never seen yourself as much of an outdoorsy type, don't feel like you have to push yourself hugely, but do see if you enjoy taking a gentle stroll among the bluebells in spring or stamping about in the frost and snow in the winter. Something about being outside makes you feel a lot more connected to the place you're living in, because you're not just surrounded by concrete and bricks and IKEA end tables. You can find native trees, rivers that travel through the country and local wildlife that's lived where you're standing for thousands of years.

This might all sound very dull to you, but I can't overstate how wonderful it feels to find yourself in a place where the only noise is birds having arguments, or a ridiculously picturesque waterfall, or wind in the trees. Give it a try.

IT'S ALMOST AS GOOD AS NANDO'S.

I will give
myself time
to rest ...

WINSTON
CHURCHILL TOOK
A NAP EVERY DAY
AND HE WAS
ALLOWED TO BE
PRIME MINISTER

I t's great to be busy, right? If you're constantly on the go, working on lots of projects and spending time with lots of people, that probably means you're important and in demand. People can't get enough of you! You barely have time to breathe, let alone have a weekend off or take a luxuriously long poo!

Since I've well and truly become an adult (past the age of twenty-five I don't think you're allowed to pretend it's not happening any more) I've noticed that a lot of people (myself included) like to talk a lot about how busy they are. We roll our eyes and sigh, but deep down we feel satisfied that our lives are *so full*, that we have so much work to do and we're so good at socialising that we never have to spend an evening alone.

The problem with this approach to life is that even if you're an extrovert, constantly being busy will eventually take its toll. Everybody has different thresholds for this. I'm sure those of you who most definitely aren't extroverts will have read the above in horror, wondering why on earth anyone would plan a week for themselves where they didn't get to have a night in.

No matter where your threshold is, at some point if you're doing too much for your own body or brain, you will reach breaking point,

AT SOME POINT IF YOU'RE DOING TOO MUCH FOR YOUR OWN BODY OR BRAIN, YOU WILL REACH BREAKING POINT and that moment won't be pretty. You might not necessarily crash and burn and find yourself standing in Sainsbury's sobbing because you can't work out what kind of bread flour you need (not that this has ever happened to me, of course) but you might find yourself feeling exhausted, irritable, in poor mental or physical health, generally run-down – basically experiencing or approaching burnout.

Taking time to rest, switch your brain off and focus on yourself shouldn't be something that you see as taking a break from life or slacking off. It should be factored into

CHECK IN
WITH YOURSELF
OFTEN

your schedule in the same way that time to sleep and take showers is. You can't perform at 100 per cent when you're studying, socialising or attempting to break a world record for knitting using spaghetti if you can't remember the last time you spent a Sunday in your pyjamas watching re-runs of *Friends* and trying to decide if you're more of a Monica or a Chandler. (I'm both. I'm a Mondler.)

I've definitely been guilty of thinking that my only limit in life is how much time I physically have in the day, and I found out the hard way that it's not true. Learn to recognise the signs of exhaustion before they spiral into something worse. I ended up in bed for the majority of a month with a cocktail of five (five!) different illnesses, mostly physical but also a bit of mental illness thrown in there as a treat, all because I didn't notice what was building up.

Check in with yourself often. Work out how you're feeling – is it time to slow down or take a break entirely? It's difficult not to worry that you'll miss out on opportunities by doing this, because the FOMO is real, people. But grabbing every possible opportunity that

FOMO IS REAL, PEOPLE

floats past with both hands when you're already juggling ten other things just means that you're going to end up half-arsing everything. Whole-arse a few things, maintain balance, and if your body is telling you that you need to take some time out to eat ice cream on the sofa and only socialise with your cat,

WHO ARE YOU TO QUESTION THAT WISDOM?

I will not
be ashamed
of what's
natural ...

BEHOLD, MY
MAGNIFICENT
PERIOD!

It's hard to accept that we're all just a collection of squishy bodily fluids, organs and limbs tucked neatly into clothes so that we can walk to the shops, go to work, etc. without people seeing all our bits. But the fact of the matter is, we are.

The human body is less upfront about what's going on inside it than, for example, something like a shrimp, which some people are apparently happy to eat despite the fact that you can see their digestive tracts through their shells. Unfortunately, unlike shrimp, which I'm sure are very

WE'VE BECOME QUITE WEIRD ABOUT BEING HONEST ABOUT OUR BODILY FUNCTIONS

relaxed about it all, we've become quite weird about being honest about our bodily functions.

Take body hair, for instance. For some reason it's generally considered okay on men but not at all on women (although I've been told that being 'too hairy', or hairy in the wrong places, is definitely a thing that men get shamed for too). Despite the fact that the majority of us grow hair on and under our arms, on our faces and in the vicinity of our genital bits (I'm sorry, there's no way to say genitalia without making you flinch in horror), women are still supposed to be as hairless and slippery as adult seals.

Periods are another thing that have somehow been made out to be gross, even though they're a normal part of a lot of people's lives. Why are some people so weird about blood just because it's coming out of the downstairs zone (see, I tried again, it's pointless)? Plenty of people feel icky about blood (me included), but if someone tells you they've got a paper cut, you're unlikely to grimace, shake your head and announce that you 'don't need to hear about it' – as has been said to me in reference to periods many times in the past.

A lot of old-fashioned patriarchy goes into making these things taboo, and we've only recently begun to talk more openly about them. There have been some steps forward – just recently I saw a model in a high fashion ad sporting armpit hair. Although lots of comments were made about how disgusting she was (disgusting! For growing hair! Which we all do!), the fact that the brand was willing to use the model with hair (a normal bodily feature!) does imply that there's some progress happening somewhere.

OUR BODIES AND WHAT THEY DO NATURALLY **SHOULD NOT BE A SHAMEFUL SECRET**

Not being able to talk openly about our bodies has a more sinister side effect too, for all genders. People find it hard to visit doctors and talk about health problems associated with the parts of our bodies we tend to be secretive about, which can mean that they get worse or go untreated for far too long.

Our bodies and what they do naturally should not be a shameful secret. It's such a hard topic to broach if you're not used to discussing it, but speaking to your friends, family or even your healthcare professional about how your body works is a great thing to make into a habit. When I was at

IF YOU WANT TO BE HAIRY, **BE HAIRY!**

university I drew a diagram of the typical female crotch parts (I'M SORRY) because some friends weren't 100 per cent sure where the different holes were, and we got to have an open chat about how bodies work. It was honestly brilliant, and I think we all learned something.

When it comes to making choices about your body that have previously been dictated by shame, your only limit should be what you personally feel comfortable with. If you want to be hairy, be hairy! There is nothing gross, unclean or unfeminine about embracing what happens when you ditch razors or waxing, nothing lazy about growing grey hairs and nothing scruffy about letting a beard grow wild and free.

I will not talk about my period in hushed tones and I will not shave just because angry commenters on the Internet are horrified by a woman with body hair. I'll do what I want, because I want to do it,

AND I HOPE YOU WILL TOO.

My true self is beautiful ...

AND TRUE SELFIES ARE HARD TO FIND ON INSTAGRAM

Have you ever wondered how people on social media manage to look so toned and fit? How they have perfectly smooth skin, impeccable make-up and eyebrows that always look as if they've been drawn on by some kind of god of facial hairs?

Spoiler alert: it's photo editing, filters and angles. Mystery solved.

I'll accept that occasionally people just manage to stand in the exact right light, on a great hair day, glowing with a genuinely amazing smile because seconds earlier they were told that their least favourite celebrity has been voted off a reality show – but this is rare.

For the most part, people have simply worked out how to look their best on the Internet. If you haven't quite mastered these tricks, or have no desire to, it can be a bit disheartening to feel like everybody else has rock-hard butt muscles and perfectly coiffed man-buns while you're foolishly looking like a normal human being.

SPOILER ALERT: IT'S PHOTO EDITING, FILTERS AND ANGLES

Before there was Instagram, we got our daily dose of 'perfect' faces and bodies from fashion models, TV presenters and the packaging for spot creams. This was at times frustrating, but sort of to be expected, as they were being paid to look nice and trick you into purchasing things. Now I think the issue is that we see ordinary people – maybe even people we know – posting the same kinds of pictures, and it can make us feel a bit inadequate and slug-like in comparison.

If everybody posted pictures of how they really look when they first wake up, when they've eaten a salad full of little mystery green things that get stuck in everybody's teeth, or when they're lying on the sofa eight episodes into a *Queer Eye* marathon (eight hours after they should have really had a shower), we'd probably all heave sighs of relief.

FOR THE MOST PART, PEOPLE HAVE SIMPLY WORKED OUT HOW **TO LOOK THEIR BEST ON THE INTERNET**

We see ourselves looking great on a regular basis (if you don't think you look great please turn back to page 106 and read it again – you are amazing). But you also see yourself at your most tired and vulnerable, post-break-ups and pre-hairbrushing, so if you're comparing that version of yourself to the carefully crafted Instagram versions of everybody else, of course there's going to be an imbalance! But you too could look just as great with the right combination of evening sunlight and editing apps.

If posting well-posed photos of yourself online will help to boost your self-esteem, you do you – but there's nothing wrong with wanting to add a bit of realism to people's newsfeeds by uploading your unedited face (gasp!), or with eschewing the practice altogether.

I'll talk in a lot more depth about the highs and lows of social media later on in this book, but I'd definitely recommend unfollowing people who make you feel bad about yourself, even if that's not at all their fault or intention. I'd go as far as to suggest deleting apps from your phone if they help you fall into unhealthy patterns of thinking about yourself and your body.

Keep things in perspective, try not to get too caught up in how other people present themselves online, and always look out for the not-so-subtle signs of photo editing for a helpful reality check – is that wall in the background meant to be curvy?

HAS HE ACCIDENTALLY SMOOTHED AWAY HALF HIS EYEBROW?!

You only get one brain

Y ou're alone, it's quiet – it's just you and your brain. Have you ever experienced that feeling when you are suddenly tempted to punch yourself right in the hippocampus just to shut it up? Or maybe you're out in the world surrounded by people when your brain decides that you're actually in the middle of a dangerous stampede, like that tragic scene in *The Lion King*, and starts sending 'Quick! RUN FROM THE ANTELOPE!' signals to your legs?

Learning how to harness the power of your brain for good rather than evil is a process, but mindfulness, self-care and knowing when to ask for help can give it a gentle kick in the right direction. Also, that video of the person lying on the ground covered in fluffy puppies. Have you seen it? Google 'covered in puppies'. Right now.

You're welcome.

Today is going
to be an
excellent day ...

FOR SOMEBODY,
AND I'D REALLY
RATHER IT
WERE ME

ou are in control of your own destiny today. I know how gross that sounds, but it's true. There are so many things in life we don't have control over, and mental health is one of those things. But we are in charge of how we react to what life throws at us. That doesn't mean I'm going to tell you that even if you're feeling bad, you must get up and go for a rousing walk, join a yoga class or create an abstract papier mâché sculpture of a dream you had last week – those things are not going to be realistic if you've woken up in a terrible state of mind.

WE ARE IN CHARGE OF HOW WE REACT TO WHAT LIFE THROWS AT US

Sometimes a successful day means that you got lots done and spent time with friends and experimented with crafts. But on days when it's hard to be a person there are lots of little things that should be celebrated as tiny victories. If you don't have the energy to celebrate them with satisfied smiles and questionable dance moves, a quiet, internal *Hooray!* will do.

Here is a list of things I would recommend for increasing the likelihood of a good day:

Treat your senses. No, this is not the tagline for luxury chocolate or budget perfume (I mean it probably is, but it's not JUST that). Your senses are battered with so many things every day, especially if you live in a city, and it can actually be really soothing just to focus in

on some individual positive sensory experiences. Smell something nice that has good associations for you (for me, this would probably be the delicate scent of frying potatoes). Touch something soft, rough or satisfyingly smooth. Put something that tastes great in your mouth. Pull up a website where you can listen to the sound of rain, or the sea, or a crackling fire, or listen to them all at the same time and imagine you're on a seaside package holiday in Wales.

Drink water. I know this is the dullest advice out of Dullsville, and water isn't magically going to solve all your problems and clear up your skin and hold you close at night when you're lonely, but water is important. When I'm feeling awful, especially if I've had a good cry, I often realise that I haven't been hydrating properly and have probably become a shrivelled human raisin on the inside (which I doubt is good for your mental or physical wellbeing).

If you're going to make it outside today, that's great, but if not, make your space inside as nice as you can. Cleaning your room might be way beyond your capabilities right now, but just making your bed and lighting a candle can turn your living space from a sadness dungeon you feel trapped inside of into a cosy den you're choosing to hide away in for a while.

Make a plan for the future. I don't mean a five-year plan that sets out exactly when you'd like to get a promotion, move cities and adopt a house-hedgehog. Just one plan that you can look forward to in the next week or month. This could be going for a nice walk, seeing a film you're looking forward to, hanging out with your friends or family. Whatever it is that makes you happy and perks you up, make that a part of your life in the near future.

Reach out to somebody. Life can be a lonely thing sometimes, and unless you love spending time by yourself without anyone around to spoil it, having an interaction with another human being could be the deciding factor between feeling good or bad about your day. A text or a phone call or even a tweet might make all the difference.

Above all else, don't beat yourself up about having a bad day. Sometimes you can try all your usual tricks and nothing can get you out of your funk. But the good news is that tomorrow is a completely new day, and you've got a fresh shot at making it okay, or good,

OR MAYBE EVEN EXCELLENT.

I am at peace
with everybody
today ...

EVEN THE
COLD CALLERS

I hate people is probably up there in the top twenty phrases I say most often, even though it's not at all true. People are a wide-ranging, nuanced bunch, and most of them are actually rather good. When I say this I usually mean that I hate crowded trains, or tourists who stop suddenly in the street so I trip over their suitcases, or someone on Twitter who just said something mean about my cat. My cat is perfection. Only the devil incarnate would disagree.

MY CAT IS PERFECTION. ONLY THE DEVIL INCARNATE WOULD DISAGREE

It's true that people can be frustrating at times, and anger and frustration are very normal emotions – but I also know I'm definitely too quick to jump to anger and I'm not alone in this. Anger is a bit of a rush at first. You become all giddy and red in the face, you get to do some great swearing or some top notch angry glares, maybe you even take it out on a stress ball, or a lamp post, or by snapping at an unfortunate person in your vicinity.

Once you're done with your anger though, the red mist will fade and you'll look around in horror at the destruction you caused, like a sci-fi character who was under evil mind control and tried to kill all their friends. Hopefully you won't have actually tried to kill any of your friends, and the damage around you will only be lovely, old-fashioned emotional shrapnel. You'll end up feeling horribly guilty and wanting to apologise to every lamp post and human person you inconvenienced in your Hulk-like rage.

The advice that gets bandied around most often is actually very useful when you tell it to yourself (rather than hearing it said very condescendingly by your gymnastics teacher when you are eight and throwing a tantrum about someone getting the same sparkly leotard as you): just take a moment to breathe, and count to ten.

Imagine that you're a huge peaceful whale in the ocean opening your giant whale mouth to eat lots of krill – except your whale mouth is your human mouth, and the krill is a big gulp of fresh air. Repeat that, and see how you're feeling.

IF YOU WANT TO FEEL MAD (OR CAN'T HELP IT) **THEN GO FOR IT**

If someone has done something really awful to you or someone else or an innocent flock of pigeons, getting angry and letting them know you're mad can feel good. But even then, in the heat of the moment, you usually don't quite get it right. A man in a suit once cut in front of me in a coffee shop, and I went up to him to tell him that there was a queue. He looked me up and down and laughed with pure derision at the idea that he should have to wait with everyone else, which incensed me so much that all I could get out was, 'You are RUDE!' before storming off a few feet back to my place in line. In retrospect, I had a great deal more to say!

Regardless of the situation, when we give in to anger we often end up looking and feeling like knobs. We recognise it when other people are taking their anger out on us because it feels horrible, but we sometimes can't see it when we're taking it out on other people – and it can hurt

LEARNING TO LET THINGS GO AND PICK YOUR BATTLES IS A VERY VALUABLE SKILL

even if it's just a general grumpy demeanour rather than a full-on gymnastics tantrum. It can be extremely difficult to do, but learning to let things go and pick your battles is a very valuable skill (and one that I haven't quite managed to master yet). There are definitely some things worth getting angry about in this world – but I reckon most everyday annoyances aren't.

At the end of the day, you're the one who has to experience and live with the anger you feel, not the people who are pissing you off, so you're the one who's suffering. If you want to feel mad (or can't help it) then go for it – but try not to take it out on those around you, and

TRY TO SAVE THE PROPER RAGE FOR ONLY THE MOST SPECIAL OF OCCASIONS.

I can face whatever today throws at me ...

IT HAS TERRIBLE AIM, ANYWAY

Some days it genuinely feels like all of the forces in the world — luck, gravity, the Force from *Star Wars* — are colluding to make you miserable. Sometimes nothing bad has even happened yet, but you fall gracefully out of bed already feeling like going outside will be a mistake.

If your brain chemistry is giving you hell or things seem like they're sliding downhill, it's really hard not to feel overwhelmed, angsty and generally negative about the curse of being a human person. On days like this I often glare at my cat and wonder if she realises that she has it so easy — conveniently forgetting that she also has to watch me clip my toenails and she has to lick her own bum to get clean.

I find that the trick to getting through a day (or week, or month) like this revolves

IN REALITY, YOU'RE WELL EQUIPPED TO DEAL WITH **MOST OF THE NONSENSE LIFE THROWS AT YOU**

around breaking life down into manageable chunks. This is something that we often do with revision, cleaning, or large bars of chocolate, but for some reason don't tend to apply to life in general. Instead of looking at your day and panicking about everything there is to do, or looking ahead to the future and only being able to see the grey fog of a joyless existence, focus on the smaller things.

Today might feel insurmountable, but if you can manage to

get through your morning to lunchtime you can treat yourself with a walk, some cake or watching an episode of the TV show that soothes you the most (mine, despite how problematic it can be, is *Friends*). If somebody throws something horrible your way, like an unexpected deadline, a sad video of a swan getting stuck in a traffic cone or a mean text that insults your grammar and puts you in a terrible mood, it often feels like it just adds to the stack of bad things and turns it into a rotten, insurmountable mountain.

I WRITE DOWN LISTS OF THE THINGS THAT ARE BOTHERING ME OR THAT I HAVE TO FACE UP TO, LIKE AN EMOTIONAL SHOPPING LIST

In reality, you're well equipped to deal with most of the nonsense life throws at you. It's just a case of taking a deep breath, a businesslike sip of water, and then tackling things one at a time. Sometimes I write down lists of the things that are bothering me or that I have to face up to, like an emotional shopping list, and even the act of writing them down can be really helpful. It's hard to have perspective when you see things as a messy mountain of bad things. But when they're written down you can work out exactly what needs to take priority, which things you might need help with and which things are actually not worth your time and mental energy and so can be scribbled off the list entirely.

It might seem like a foolish dream for me to say that you can just decide not to be upset or worried about something, but to some extent we do have a choice about how we react to challenges in life. You can't control everything that happens to you, but you can control how you choose to deal with it, and in some circumstances, that might mean choosing not to deal with it at all. I decided not to let somebody at work bother me, and then focused on that every time they popped up to say something infuriating, and eventually it came true – they weren't bothering me. I tricked myself into having a more chill existence on earth! Brains are so silly!

At the end of the day, the day has to end. I've either just written something very wise by saying that or very ridiculous. But either way, it's true. You can take things one day at a time, and remember – everything always seems worse at night, and a little bit brighter in the morning.

EVEN BOOK DEADLINES.

I am comfortable in my own company ...

I'M THE ONE PERSON, LIVING OR DEAD, I'D LIKE TO HAVE DINNER WITH

If I'm left alone for too long, my inner monologue starts screaming the sad songs from *Les Misérables* and won't shut up. I'm a grown woman who panics if she hasn't got any plans with friends coming up, talks to her cat about it for a few hours, then makes plans every night for the next two weeks to overcompensate and ends up completely exhausted and wishing she had a week free, with no social engagements, to relax.

Lots of people can find it very tough to feel comfortable in their own company. Although being an extrovert has many benefits when it comes to dealing with other people, I do hugely envy anyone who can look at an entire weekend stretching ahead of them with no plans outside their duvet without feeling existential panic and deciding they've got no friends and will die alone covered in pizza sauce.

THE TIME YOU GET TO SPEND IN YOUR OWN COMPANY SHOULD BE PRECIOUS, NOT A BURDEN

In fact the time you get to spend in your own company should be precious, not a burden. A lot of being comfortable on your own is about re-framing it in your brain, so that instead of seeing it as time spent *without* people or plans, you think of it as being time spent *with* yourself, or working on your own plans.

Next time you have a free night or weekend, instead of worrying that it means you're doomed to friendlessness

OUR INNER MONOLOGUES **AREN'T ALWAYS KIND TO US**

forever, think about all the things you don't usually have time or the capacity to do – now is the time to do them!

Our inner monologues aren't always kind to us. I've definitely experienced the late-night worries about life and what I'm doing with mine, while I sit fully clothed in bed at 1 a.m. knowing it's time to brush my teeth but unable to motivate myself for oral hygiene. Try being positive about yourself, even if it feels forced at first. And if it's the middle of the night when things always seem crapper, please just try to get some sleep.

Make the most of the time you get to spend with yourself! Whether you start building a tiny model replica of the town you live in, take an

IF IT'S THE MIDDLE OF THE NIGHT WHEN THINGS ALWAYS SEEM CRAPPER, PLEASE JUST TRY TO GET SOME SLEEP

hour-long bath with nine bath bombs or choose to indulge in something totally, deliciously mindless so you can properly switch off and recharge for the next time you need to be around people, that time is precious and you shouldn't wish it away.

And if all else fails, you're still lonely and you've got a lot of attention and energy you need to offload

JUST ADOPT
A HAMSTER

somewhere, just adopt a hamster. The hamster is your best friend now. He'll never let you down, but he will poo in your hand.

WHAT A LEGEND.

I will make time
to meditate and
be mindful ...

AND TRY NOT TO
BRAG TOO MUCH
ABOUT IT
AT BRUNCH

meditation has weird connotations. I know I definitely imagined that you couldn't really meditate unless you were a Buddhist monk, or you were on one of those meditation retreats where they don't let you use your phone or talk to anybody. (These are real and my friend has gone on one. He said it was quite nice, but I know if I did it I'd get 'Jingle Bells' stuck in my head in the first ten minutes and run screaming from the retreat on the second day.)

Meditation in the way that I experience it isn't about clearing your mind or transcending this world for another one where you're just an insignificant pale blue speck (I feel insignificant and speck-like enough in my regular conscious life, thank you very much), and it's not about spirituality or religion either (although, of course, that doesn't mean it can't be if that's what you're into).

I DEFINITELY IMAGINED THAT YOU COULDN'T REALLY MEDITATE **UNLESS YOU WERE A BUDDHIST MONK**

The basic concept of mindfulness meditation involves learning how to bring your attention back to what's happening in the current moment. That's it. It may not sound like much, but try to go ten seconds without your mind wandering off and thinking about your to-do list or what you want for dinner, and you will see for yourself that it isn't as easy as it sounds.

I seem to have gone off on a tangent – this is what our minds naturally do. But mindfulness meditation doesn't punish you for doing that, or ever imagine that you'd be able to keep things like *Bugsy Malone* out of your mind – it's about noticing every time your mind wanders, and bringing it back to the present moment.

LEARNING TO BE PRESENT IN THE MOMENT IS A SKILL **THAT CAN HELP YOU IN ALL SORTS OF SITUATIONS**

I'm not going to try to explain the entire process of mindfulness, as I'm sure I'd get it wrong and there are many books, apps and free websites that will teach you the basics and can provide you with guided meditations to get you into it (I use *Calm* and *Headspace,* which you can get on your phone – or the free guided meditations from the UCLA Health website). What I can do is vouch for the fact that it can really help with anxiety, negative thought spirals, or times when you're so stressed you can't remember the last time you had the luxury of a poo.

Learning to be present in the moment is a skill that can help you in all sorts of situations. I often feel that I spend so much time anticipating things both positive and negative, imagining how they'll turn out, and then suddenly they've happened and they're already memories – and I've missed the thing I was spending all that time thinking about in the first place.

Making ten minutes of time every day to sit with yourself and try mindfulness meditation is definitely worth doing. It might not be for you, and if it isn't, all you've done is experimented and spent a bit of time relaxing, which is never a bad thing. If it does turn out to be for you, there's such a weird sense of peace that comes from it that's hard to describe unless you've experienced it. I realise this sounds like some sort of induction into a cult. I promise you will at no point have to pay me to advance to the next level/ get to meditation paradise.

I REALISE THIS SOUNDS LIKE SOME SORT OF INDUCTION INTO A CULT

Try a few different methods or guided sessions and see what happens. Just imagine, if it all goes well you can be one of those people who goes to brunch and talks loudly about what amazing revelations they had during their last meditation, and how calm and in touch they feel with the world around them.

What do you mean, nobody wants to be that person? Whatever. You live your truth, I'll live mine.

PASS ME THE AVOCADO TOAST.

I refuse to
feel inferior ...

UNLESS
SPECIFICALLY TOLD
TO DO SO BY
SIR DAVID
ATTENBOROUGH

most of us like the world around us to have some sort of rule and order to it, which is why it's so satisfying to alphabetise your books or colour-code your clothes or teach your dogs to line up in size order. Unfortunately, this also means that we have a tendency to try to sort people into categories to make sense of them, which isn't always a very positive or productive thing if you don't feel like you're top of the pile. There are two different types of inferiority:

The type we talk ourselves into. We observe others and their successes, or try to measure up to some imagined version of who we should be by now, and decide we've come up short.

The kind that comes about when people make us feel inferior. Sometimes this is by accident, like when somebody solves a complicated maths problem with ease or tells you how many horses they have (and you have *no* horses). But sometimes it's on purpose.

If you consistently feel like you're not measuring up to your own idea of how you'd like to live your life, this may be worth examining. You might find that there are a few changes you want to make that will increase your general satisfaction and, while not providing you with many horses to brag about, help to keep those feelings of inadequacy at bay. Maybe you want to change jobs, or live by your morals more often, or start jogging every second Tuesday of the month in tiny Lycra shorts. These are all positive changes. Especially the shorts.

What's not positive, though, is beating yourself up about this stuff and letting it make you feel like you're 'lesser'. Your life isn't less than whatever your current ideal is – it's just different.

INSTEAD OF GETTING CAUGHT IN THE NEGATIVE CYCLE, GET CAUGHT IN A POSITIVE SPIRAL **THAT ONLY GOES UP!**

There's a very good chance that if you examine your feelings of inferiority further, you'll actually find that they're not coming from rational thoughts at all, just a general feeling of negativity that you've decided is down to your own failings. Positive changes/ Lycra shorts might help in this situation, but they're not going to fix it entirely.

Addressing this is tough, and as someone who is, as I have mentioned, very much not a qualified therapist (not even a therapist for cats, which is a thing), I can't pretend I have all the answers. But I know that when I'm feeling down, I tend to fall into negative cycles where my inner monologue gets pretty mean and personal about all my so-called failings, and repeats this nastiness until I'm at the bottom of an emotional hole.

It might make you feel like a bit of a hippy interpretive

dance life coach (apologies if that's your job, and apologies to the cat therapists too) but taking on what I'm trying to preach in this book and learning to actively repeat positive phrases about yourself rather than negative ones is a really helpful tool. Instead of getting caught in the negative cycle, get caught in a positive spiral that only goes up! Like a hurricane, but great! I have no idea if hurricanes go up, but they sure do seem excited about getting where they're going.

Instead of thinking, *I'm bad at crossword puzzles*, think, *I'm committed to improving my crossword skills!* or, *I try my best and give it my all when it comes to crossword puzzles!* Wear your approval of yourself like armour, so that even when people try to chip away at you, you're basically a human rhino:

IMPENETRABLE, STOIC AND WITH SURPRISINGLY SENSITIVE FEET.

I will not compare myself to others ...

WE CAN'T ALL BE ASTRONAUTS – SPACE WOULD BE A NIGHTMARE AT RUSH HOUR

There are some things in life that you will never be. Maybe you're never going to be an astronaut, or an opera singer, or the world's tallest DJ. If these things are your goals, I'm not saying they're totally unrealistic – you do it! Become the most tuneful, record-playing astronaut there ever was! But sometimes there are things we want that we have to accept will only ever be fantasies. When you see other people living those fantasies, it can be pretty hard not to compare your life to theirs.

WHEN YOU SEE OTHER PEOPLE LIVING THOSE FANTASIES, **IT CAN BE PRETTY HARD NOT TO COMPARE YOUR LIFE TO THEIRS**

The problem is that it's now so easy to see other people living your dream life. Back in the day we just had to imagine the exciting or glamorous things people were getting up to around the world, or hope they'd make an appearance on an MTV reality show about their lives. But now *the whole Internet* is an MTV reality show. If you want to be a bungee instructor, a dog groomer or just very, very disgustingly rich, you can find someone who's doing that and look at their social media channels until you're green with envy.

Of course, when it comes to comparing yourself to the atrociously rich, this can be a special kind of frustrating. Money can't buy you happiness, but if you're used to struggling with money, it can be a bit heart-wrenching to see other people living lives that look so much easier and feel so out of reach. This also applies to people who have natural abilities you weren't born with – some people are just naturally built to do certain things, and some people have innately terrible hand–eye coordination and would fall at the first hurdle (astronaut-wise).

WE ALL OCCASIONALLY MUTTER JEALOUSLY AS WE WATCH PEOPLE'S INCREDIBLE INSTAGRAM STORIES ON THE TOILET

We all compare ourselves to others sometimes. We've all got dreams that are just out of reach, and we all occasionally mutter jealously as we watch people's incredible Instagram stories on the toilet.

The good news is that celebrating the positive things in your own life can help you quell the jealous toilet rambling. Here's some free therapy that I stole from my actual, qualified therapist (thanks, my therapist, sorry, my therapist). If you feel like you're not appreciating the great stuff that happens to you or that you make happen, then at the end of each day or each week sit down and think about three things:

Something you're grateful for (like the weather, your health, a kindly stranger on the street who told you your hat was nice).

Something you enjoyed (an ice cream, a text from a friend, the expression on your cat's face when she accidentally fell off your bed).

Something you're satisfied with (organising your desk, finally sending an email you were putting off, getting the perfect video of your cat falling off the bed).

It's also much healthier and more fun to focus on goals you can achieve, rather than ones that other people have achieved. If certain things seem out of reach, decide on stuff you can actually work towards and dedicate your time and energy to making that happen. If you focus on yourself and look inwards rather than always looking at other people, eventually you'll glance up and realise that you don't mind what everybody else is doing, because you're crushing it in your own life.

AND THAT'S QUITE A NICE PLACE TO BE.

I'm not okay
today ...
AND THAT'S
OKAY. OKAY?

Ahhh, positivity. Looking on the bright side, a constant perky disposition, finding the silver lining. Irritating sometimes, isn't it?

I am all for trying to be positive. I may have even recommended it many times in this book. But sometimes you're just not okay. And no matter how many positive affirmations and helpful tips from fortune cookies you read, your day can't be fixed. This is not some kind of failure on your part. Unlike what many lifestyle gurus and juice cleanse advocates might try to tell you, it's not always possible to think yourself happy. Feeling bad is just part of being a person, and more so for some than for others.

IT'S NATURAL TO ALWAYS **TRY TO FIX PROBLEMS**

It's natural to always try to fix problems. Birds do it, apes do it, and I have no evidence of this but I'm sure sea monkeys are working hard to sort things out in their little plastic universes. I notice this in the people around me, and in myself too. If someone I love is having a bad day, I'll try to find a way to solve their issues practically. And if I'm having a tough time, the good eggs in my life will often try to tell me that everything is all right or can be sorted out. The problem is that this isn't always what you need to hear.

Sometimes we don't need our problems to be solved in a logical way, because often we're not feeling bad about things that can really be solved simply. Maybe it seems like you're upset because you left your favourite mittens on a bus, but you're actually just generally bummed out about the injustices of the world. The offer to buy you new mittens might help a little, but it doesn't get rid of your general woes and grievances with life.

IT'S OKAY TO CREATE A BLANKET FORT IN YOUR BED AND STAY IN IT ALL DAY

The thing to remember is … it's okay to feel bad.

It may not be fun, but it's certainly not something you should beat yourself up for or feel guilty about. It's okay to create a blanket fort in your bed and stay in it all day, eating plain slices of bread and ignoring your phone. Equally, it's okay to be too sad to even think about building something as complex as a blanket fort or buying sliced bread. As always, if you're feeling bad a little too often and it's affecting your life, I recommend speaking to somebody (remember that there is a list of resources at the front of this book), but having bad days now and then is completely normal.

I've mentioned this before,

THE THING TO REMEMBER IS … IT'S OKAY TO FEEL BAD

but it's also okay if you experience sadness in different ways to other people, or if you need different kinds of support (or prefer no support at all) when you're struggling. It's best to try to communicate as much as possible with the people around you about what you need. Try doing it when you're feeling good so you're not weighed down by the grey blanket of glumness. That way, when the time comes, they know what to do without you even having to ask.

It's true that your bad feelings will pass, but until they do, don't put pressure on yourself to cheer up when it's just not going to happen today. Settle down with whatever keeps you going in times like this, allow yourself to be a bit selfish so you can focus on coping however you do it best, and re-emerge from your chrysalis when you're ready, as a little baby butterfly –

SLIGHTLY EXHAUSTED, BUT VERY MUCH ALIVE.

It's good to ask
for help ...

WHILE CARRYING
HEAVY STUFF
IN YOUR ARMS OR
IN YOUR HEAD

*O*nce when I was trying to carry heavy bags of groceries home from the shops at university, my flatmate asked if I needed any help. I responded, 'No! I'm a strong, independent, confident woman, and I don't need help!' About ten minutes later I had to call him back and say, 'I'm still a strong, independent, confident

SOMETIMES IT'S JUST REALLY HARD TO ASK FOR HELP

woman, but I very much do need help if I want my arms to stay attached to my body. And I do, Daniel. I do.'

I think you can see where I'm going with this. Sometimes it's just really hard to ask for help. It feels like needing other people is a weakness, or proves that you're not equipped to deal with your own life, or that maybe you shouldn't have bought ten cans of chickpeas if you were going to have to carry all your shopping home by yourself (but they're just so good! They're nature's Pringles).

Some people find this harder than others. I'm lucky in that I've been conditioned by rubbish traditional gender roles to feel like it's okay to talk openly about my feelings and rely on others emotionally. For lots of people (especially men) it's much harder, due to years of being told that it's a sign of strength to suck it up, suffer in silence and only express feelings in the form of rage aimed at malfunctioning vending machines and delayed commuter trains. The other day I actually heard a middle-aged man shout, out loud, to HIMSELF, 'Will this f*!?ing train ever get to London?'

It's probably not entirely his fault. It's likely that he hasn't been taught how to express himself in other ways, or that it's okay to lean on his friends and family when times are tough and the train seems like it'll never make it to London. Even those of us who are used to spilling our guts out when work is hard or we've seen a pigeon who only has one foot (how can we help them? Their lives are so hard!) sometimes struggle with feeling like our problems are too silly, or too hard to talk about with anyone else. But believe me, nobody is going to feel burdened by you if you need help, or a shoulder to leave snot on, or just a friend to watch episodes of *Brooklyn Nine-Nine* with until life hurts a bit less.

NOBODY IS GOING TO FEEL BURDENED BY YOU IF YOU NEED HELP, OR A SHOULDER TO LEAVE SNOT ON

The other kind of help we find it very hard to ask for is the kind that even the best of friends usually aren't able to offer as part of the smorgasbord of their friendship – professional help. Just like any other part of your body, your brain gets ill, and when that happens it makes perfect sense to see a doctor or a therapist.

I strongly believe that pretty much everybody could benefit from a little bit of therapy, and the more openly we talk about it, the less people will feel like it's weird or gross or something only people from LA who own yoga studios would do. If you had a wound that wouldn't stop bleeding, you wouldn't think, *It would be a sign of weakness for me to ask for help with this – it'll sort itself out!* Actually, the guy on the train probably would. I hope you're reading this book, my man. If you ever need to have a good cry about pigeon welfare,

YOU JUST GIVE ME A CALL.

The robots work for you now

Social media and smartphones open up a vast and previously unexplored landscape of potential to make friends, discover new things and embarrass yourself so thoroughly that you beg your dog to swap lives with you (even though you've seen him eat his own poo).

It could be argued that eating one's own poo is preferable to liking someone's Instagram photo from 181 days ago, posting something private to the completely wrong account, or daring to talk about politics on the Internet and then getting hate-tweets from twelve men who all have default profile pictures and are all called Dave. The Internet is fun, isn't it?

My life is wonderful, but it's not perfect ...

AND ANYBODY WHO SAYS THEIRS IS MUST BE BLUFFING

Would it actually be nice to always have perfectly clean, fresh sheets, complicated quinoa-porridge breakfasts, meticulously toned abs and a French bulldog puppy you could dress up in Christmas jumpers? The big names of Instagram sell this to us as the dream … but let's break it down.

THERE'LL BE EVEN MORE LAUNDRY WHEN YOU INEVITABLY SPILL THAT LATTE ON THOSE SHEETS

Unless you become a millionaire overnight, you're going to have to do all the hard work behind the scenes yourself. You've got to constantly do laundry to make sure your bed looks nice for the next 'lazy Sunday in bed #soblessed' picture. You've got to buy a proper coffee machine so you can steam the almond milk for the latte you'll be placing precariously on a knitted blanket on top of those sheets. There'll be even more laundry when you inevitably spill that latte on those sheets.

Making quinoa-infused porridge with home-made nut butter and berry compote for breakfast takes a lot of time and money spent at the organic food shop. You'll be giving up your lunch break every day to go to the gym in exchange for the abs, which frankly sounds exhausting, and spending all your money on flights to exotic locales (which will really cut into your nut butter budget).

Your French bulldog puppy will have been horribly overbred and will barely be able to breathe through its little snout, so you'd better start saving to treat its expensive health problems in later life. I know. I'm a right little ray of sunshine.

PRESENTING YOUR LIFE AS PERFECT ON SOCIAL MEDIA
IS ALMOST A FULL-TIME JOB

The point I'm trying to make is that presenting your life as perfect on social media is almost a full-time job in itself. Everybody's actually using filters to make their sheets whiter, cropping out the messy parts of their bedrooms, and spending so long making their fancy breakfasts that they're late for work and barely have time to eat said fancy breakfast.

The only people who really do have effortlessly Instagram-ready lives are the über-wealthy, with staff to make their breakfast and their beds. And as much as it pains me to say this, you could have *twenty* pugs and it wouldn't guarantee happiness. I know, it sounds unlikely. But it's true.

Scrolling through post after post of supposed perfection and then looking around at your own situation – maybe your duvet cover doesn't match your rug, maybe you ate a banana and some Marmite toast for breakfast, maybe your dog is just a regular dog with healthy DNA from lots of lovely randomised cross-breeding – can make you feel a bit deflated. Marmite is, of course, widely known as the least Instagrammable spread.

But the most wonderful parts of your life are probably the ones that wouldn't look good on Instagram anyway. I for one have had some of the best times of my life holding a slice of Marmite toast.

I doubt people will ever stop putting on a show for social media. As long as people enjoy pictures of perfectly organised desks with a single cactus for decoration, Instagrammers everywhere will be sweeping their real work things into a drawer and arranging that cactus just so to get the killer photo. Now that it's possible to make money out of having an aesthetically pleasing life, there's even more motivation to pretend you don't have a pair of yesterday's underwear crumpled on the floor just out of frame.

THE MOST WONDERFUL PARTS OF YOUR LIFE ARE PROBABLY THE ONES THAT WOULDN'T LOOK GOOD ON INSTAGRAM

If you worked really hard to create moments where it *appears* you have a perfect life, then you could have an Instagram account like that too. But who's got the time? And let's face it, it's pretty unlikely that when you're older you'll be thinking, *I wish I'd spent less time out there living my messy, wonderful life and more time taking pictures of scented candles on a piece of marble wrapping paper disguised to look like*

AN EXPENSIVE TABLE.

My self-worth
is not measured in
followers ...

IT'S MEASURED IN
HOW MANY DOGS
SMILED AT ME
TODAY

I f you post a picture of you and your friends hanging out by a fallen tree in a forest and nobody is around to 'like' it, does it still make a sound? If your thoughts about politics and witty observations about Eurovision are only read by your twelve Twitter followers, does that make them less important?

In this shiny new world of online 'influencers', it can be disheartening to watch your genuinely good jokes and pictures of your dog flop on the Internet while someone with millions of followers can accidentally post gibberish because they've sat on their phone, and get instant adoration. The way that things are

SORT OF LIKE HENRY THE VIII'S COURT
BUT WITH BLOCKINGS AND UNFOLLOWINGS INSTEAD OF BEHEADINGS

structured online – with algorithms making the successful more successful, and some accounts crowned as the most important with a verified status – creates a social hierarchy that's sort of like Henry the VIII's court but with blockings and unfollowings instead of beheadings.

Being told not to measure your worth in numbers is all well and good, except that the world continues to do it for us: how much we earn, how many steps we walk a day and how many people retweet our witty take on the new royal baby's name are all counted and presented to us on the regular. Aside from just the comparisons to how everybody else is doing online, there's also that rush that comes with getting likes or retweets. It's the kind of instant validation that usually only comes when everybody in a group you're hanging out with cracks up at your joke.

But have you ever noticed how much harder people laugh at a joke if it's being made by somebody considered really important that they're trying to impress? I bet the Queen could make a rubbish Christmas cracker joke and everybody around her would be in stitches. The social media content that people with big followings put out on the Internet isn't necessarily better or worthier of respect. It's just seen by *a lot* of people, who are eager to be noticed by their number one bae.

THERE ARE MUCH MORE IMPORTANT THINGS TO MEASURE YOUR LIFE IN

People post things online for many reasons, and getting lots of likes and followers doesn't have to be one of them. We're sharing our experience of the world, our thoughts on the things that matter and our jokes about the things that don't. We're creating a digital identity for ourselves and a scrapbook of our lives to look back on. We're learning and discovering new content and communities, and we're connecting with people we would otherwise never meet. All of these things sound much more positive and fulfilling than just getting a lot of retweets, which at the most might land you with some intense followers and a morally questionable sponsorship deal with Coca-Cola.

What's more, nobody who actually knows you is going to base their opinion on how important you are on the Internet. Not even a little bit. No person you want to spend time with is writing up an invite list for their birthday party and crossing off anybody who has fewer than a hundred Twitter followers.

There are much more important things to measure your life in. Like, as mentioned above, how many dogs you managed to meet today. If you're afraid of dogs, please do cross out the word 'dogs' in that sentence and replace with an appropriate animal.

I HEAR THAT SQUIRRELS ARE ALSO EXCELLENT JUDGES OF CHARACTER.

I will spread love, not war ...

EVEN WHEN IT COMES TO ANONYMOUS TWITTER TROLLS CALLED DAVE

The Internet is nice, isn't it? Where else can you go at such short notice to have people tell you you're ugly, irrelevant and your ideas are stupid? It's a service, really.

It's a well-known phenomenon that people are often a lot crueller online than they are in person. It's easier to say awful things when you don't have to stand in front of a real person to say them. It's even easier if you're operating anonymously so it looks like it's a perky anime character telling you that they hope you die in a blazing fire.

IT'S EASIER TO SAY AWFUL THINGS WHEN YOU DON'T HAVE TO STAND IN FRONT OF A REAL PERSON TO SAY THEM

When somebody's saying awful things to you for fun, or because they have a different political opinion to you, or maybe because they take *Harry Potter* very seriously and think you're fatally wrong about which characters should have ended up married (a real thing people have been very angry with me about in the past), your instinct is to defend yourself. The same boldness that the other person is getting from behind a monitor might also bless you with a superhuman ability to stand up for yourself, and suddenly you have the courage you never had in the playground when people were saying you looked like a frog.

I'm not going to tell you that you shouldn't stand up for yourself, or that you should always ignore bullies. But the saying 'don't feed the trolls' does sometimes apply when somebody's genuinely attacking you out of nowhere just to get a rise out of you.

The thing to remember is that no matter how awful they're being at that moment in time, there is a human person sitting somewhere sending thinly veiled insults or using that crying-laughing emoji to get you all riled up. If they're just being plain old nasty, there's probably something going on with them in their life that's making them this way, and if they're arguing a point you disagree with then they probably feel just as certain that they're in the right as you do.

THEY MIGHT NOT BE SO FOND OF YOU IF THEY SEE THAT YOU CALLED SOMEBODY A RAGING MORON BECAUSE THEY DIDN'T ENJOY A *STAR WARS* FILM THAT YOU LOVED

Trust me, you might feel good for ten seconds after you send a scathing, biting response that rips their argument to shreds or frustrates them to their core, but you know what doesn't feel good? Imagining the actual person on the other end seeing your reply, letting out a sigh and feeling a bit sad.

Go a little further – push your empathy button and imagine they're alone in their darkened flat with only some old carrots and low-fat margarine in their fridge, weeping gently as Coldplay quietly serenade them in the background.

Feel free to argue, debate, stand up for yourself – but don't do it in a way that you'll feel ashamed of the next day. And remember – potential friends and employers can also read these tweets, and they might not be so fond of you if they see that you called somebody a raging moron because they didn't enjoy a *Star Wars* film that you loved. As much as you can, try to take a deep breath and step away from the Internet for at least an hour before you respond – by then, the whole thing might seem a little trivial.

As with most things, this isn't a clear-cut black and white issue and there are sometimes mitigating circumstances. It's not right to police the anger or tone of people who've been oppressed all their lives for their gender, sexuality, race or identity, when somebody's trying to continue that oppression by being vile on the Internet. Whether or not you think their approach is the most constructive or healthy is irrelevant if you haven't also experienced that same oppression, because you can't imagine what it's like to live that person's life and be worn down by anonymous trolls called Dave on the regular.

Just keep on reminding yourself that we're all people –

AND THINK ABOUT THAT SAD, SAD COLDPLAY SONG PLAYING ON INTO THE NIGHT.

I will be
thoughtful
about the footprint
I leave behind ...

NOW, WHAT WAS
MY OLD MYSPACE
PASSWORD?

In films and books about the olden days, people seemed very concerned about what kind of physical mark they were going to leave on this earth. Not to bum you out, but it's true that one day you'll be gone and everybody who knew you will be gone. Back in ye olden times it seems that everybody was trying to write their memoirs or work out how to get someone to paint a portrait of them so they could glare down upon their ancestors for evermore.

WHILE OUR GRANDKIDS LAUGH AT US AND SEND MEAN MESSAGES ABOUT US OVER THEIR INTEGRATED BRAIN CHIPS

The world is a very different place now. In a few hundred years, when people are wondering what it is that an ordinary person might have done on a rainy Tuesday in 2018, they'll just be able to look up the Facebook archives. 'Ah, yes, you see here? Jack was putting lots of little hats on his cat. And Jenny was wondering if you can eat spaghetti six months after the use-by date.'

Technology is changing so rapidly that by the time we're all old, we'll probably still be trying to use Instagram filters and order takeaway through mobile phone apps while our grandkids laugh at us and send mean messages about us over their integrated brain chips. But there's also a good chance that a lot of what we put out on the Internet might stick around for a while. You may have heard people talk about 'Internet footprints', which can be defined as everything that can be discovered about us through the information we've made available online.

I feel a little thrill of horror every time I remember that the slightly saucy piece of *Harry Potter* fanfiction I

THINKING ABOUT WHAT WE'RE LEAVING IN OUR WAKE ON THE INTERNET
CAN ALSO MEAN POSITIVE CHANGE

wrote eleven years ago is still out there somewhere, probably long since unread but impossible to delete as I have no idea where it is now. I was using the Internet heavily from the age of about twelve and I expect people younger than me start even earlier than that. I dread to think what mean forum comments twelve-year-old me was writing about people who didn't appreciate the true pain and artistry of Avril Lavigne.

Taking control of your online footprint mostly means making everything as private as possible. Check your privacy settings and then check them again. Then think carefully about what you do decide to make public. Nobody's perfect, but I'm not sure I'd feel too great about my granddaughter looking up from her personal holographic screen to say, 'Grandma, why did you call somebody a "piece of crap" in 2007 because they didn't like a television show called *Scrubs*?'

When the historians of tomorrow stumble upon you, do you want them to think, 'Yikes, really aggressive tweets from this one – put them on the pile for studying how awful people were on early social media platforms'?

Thinking about what we're leaving in our wake on the Internet can also mean positive change. We've got the power to connect with people all over the world, so why not use that power to reach out to those who are struggling, or help people find the wedding rings they accidentally leave on trains, or write glowing reviews of your favourite local businesses? Trying to add more positivity to the online world will probably make you feel much fonder of the Internet in general.

I'm not saying you can't get into heated debates with people who are very wrong about your favourite television shows, but maybe do it in moderation or as a little treat,

LIKE EATING CHOCOLATE CEREAL AT THE WEEKEND.

My life is
full and
interesting ...

EVEN IF THERE'S
NO PROOF ON
SOCIAL MEDIA

When I was a teenager and I met a new person or developed a crush on someone, I'd often check out their Facebook page to see what they were like. Facebook would helpfully show me how many friends they had, their recent photos and all the weird *Family Guy*-related pages they'd liked when they were twelve – a helpful overview of who they were as a person. I remember thinking that if somebody hadn't been tagged in lots of photos recently (or ever)

I WAS VERY GUILTY OF MEASURING MY SELF-WORTH ACCORDING TO HOW I APPEARED ONLINE

then they must be a bit of an introvert, or not have many friends. I judged the entire way they interacted with society from whether or not they were uploading proof of these interactions to social media.

I did the same for myself. If I looked back at my social media profiles and I didn't seem to have been out much lately or tagged in new pictures, I'd panic and upload a bunch of grainy phone pictures of me and my friends doing something that definitely didn't need sharing, like eating a burrito on a trampoline, and sigh with relief when my feed updated and it looked like I was truly enjoying my youth. I was very guilty of measuring my self-worth according to how I appeared online, and I think sometimes I still am to an extent.

Today, if you look at someone's profile and see that there's not much going on there, you think they're probably far too busy doing interesting things to post about them, or that they really value their privacy and don't feel the need to share. But you may not apply this logic to yourself – you might still worry that people will look at the identity you've carved out online and make judgements about how cool you are, or what kind of life you're living.

DON'T FEEL THAT WITHOUT THE EVIDENCE, YOUR JOY DOESN'T EXIST

I suggest a big question to think about is why exactly you do put up pictures and update your status on social media. Maybe you're on Twitter to make people laugh and be part of a community, or on Facebook to message your friends and keep up with parties and events. Ideally, social media shouldn't be something that becomes so core to your identity that you feel constant pressure to maintain your image and presence. Social media platforms should be a tool that you use to enrich your life experience by finding out new things, interacting with people you'd otherwise never encounter and making really good jokes about Eurovision.

If you find yourself wanting to put up pictures or posts about all the fun you're having just to prove you're having it – don't! If you want to put up pictures of you having fun for other reasons, such as to share the moment with friends, archive it in some way outside your phone or build a helpful alibi for a crime you're committing – go for it! But don't feel that without the evidence, your joy doesn't exist.

I think we're always going to have varying motives for the stuff we put online, and I'm not trying to strictly police how you use social media or encourage you to do so for other people – we get enough of that from clickbait articles written by middle-aged journalists. People are always going to complain that young people live through their phones and cameras, taking pictures and videos of experiences instead of actually experiencing them. I think this is bollocks. It's perfectly natural to want to capture a moment so you can relive it or share it later. The only thing to be wary of is whether or not you're really posting pictures of your burrito/trampoline antics for yourself, or because of the pressure you feel to appear to be the queen of the burrito trampoline.

IT SHOULD ALWAYS BE MOSTLY FOR YOU.

I will be present in the moment ...

INSTEAD OF PICKING UP MY PHONE TO TELL SOMEONE HOW PRESENT I AM

S martphones are the best invention since sliced bread, which actually downplays them a bit because sliced bread seems like it was relatively easy to invent compared to the complicated technology that went into creating FaceTime. The fact that you can't get lost as long as you have phone battery, that you can communicate with people around the world at the touch of a button and that you can turn yourself into a sexy cat or dog using Instagram filters is a glorious gift to man- and womankind. In many ways I think phones have genuinely made us more social.

THAT YOU CAN TURN YOURSELF INTO A SEXY CAT OR DOG USING INSTAGRAM FILTERS IS A GLORIOUS GIFT

Technology has bridged a lot of gaps and made communication much easier. Many of us have made friends we never would have been able to otherwise, through online platforms and communities. We can find dates on dating apps and websites, rather than by staring hopefully at random people in bars and hoping they turn around and don't think you're looking at the person behind them. Presidents can tweet whatever they want and my parents have even learned how to use emojis!

The problem is that we're so used to being constantly plugged in that we reach for our phones automatically, even when we're in social situations where it's considered a bit rude to be staring at a screen. I don't know about you, but it's become my default reaction to a pause in conversation or a moment of awkwardness to pick up my phone and immediately start watching supermodels renovate their kitchens on Instagram stories. I've done it on dates, at dinner with my family, so far not while kissing someone or at a funeral but it's only a matter of time.

It took me a long time to notice I was actually doing it, even though I'd noticed other people doing it when I was trying to talk to them. Sometimes I don't mind – if I'm casually chatting to someone and they're managing to keep up their end of the conversation, I don't need 100 per cent of their concentration. But if I'm spilling my guts out about my biggest fears – flying, hurting a pigeon's feelings – and then look up with eyes brimming with tears to see someone chuckling gently at some viral tweets, I'm going to be a little annoyed.

THE MAIN THING IS TO TRY TO **MAINTAIN BALANCE**

Experiment with how long you can go without looking at your phone. Put your phone somewhere inaccessible so you can't reach for it, or don't bring it out with you if you're with someone else who has one to hand. There are lots of ways to make your phone seem less demanding or appealing too. Change the settings so it's not constantly buzzing with notifications or lighting up every time you nudge it so you get sucked into the technology portal like a shy yet curious child in a sci-fi film.

There are even apps that help you stay focused by doing things like setting limits for how long you're allowed to look at your phone each day, or by growing trees as a reward for not looking at your screen when you're meant to be working (these two are called *Moment* and *Forest*). (Is it ironic to recommend phone apps as a way to stop you from using your phone? Maybe. I'm still not fully sure what irony is. Alanis Morissette has set me back years.)

The main thing is to try to maintain balance. If you're looking at your phone a lot because you're launching an exciting new online business, or having hilarious conversations with your friends from your Ryan Gosling fan forum, I don't see anything wrong with that. But if you're looking at your phone as a default when you'd actually like to be more present in the moment, enjoying a hesitant yet sensual first kiss, for example, or celebrating the life of an obscure relative, then make a few simple changes and

GET YOUR HEAD BACK IN THE REAL WORLD.

I will step
away from
social media ...

AND LIVE WITHOUT
REFRESHING,
LIKE THEY DID
IN OLDEN TIMES

It's hard to imagine, but once upon a time, there was no social media. I know. I lived through this period of prehistory. Maybe you did too. My first experience using a computer was playing a game called *Petz*, where you had a little dog or cat made of about seven pixels that chased a ball around your desktop. These were dark times, but we made do.

They've done studies about the effects of social media, and why we keep scrolling and refreshing as naturally as we blink and breathe. Apparently we get a little rush of dopamine from opening an app and being instantly presented with a plethora of information, jokes,

I REFUSE TO DENOUNCE SOCIAL MEDIA AS **A TERRIBLE EVIL THAT IS PLAGUING YOUNG PEOPLE TODAY**

sexist hashtags and Kardashian gifs. Studies have shown that most people check their phones and social media sites within the first half an hour of waking up.

I refuse to denounce social media as a terrible evil that is plaguing young people today. Maybe because I sort of grew up on it and I think the Internet has enriched my life – I've made friends on social media, I've laughed until I've cried at a perfectly constructed tweet and I've learned more about gender, race, sexuality, class and politics online than I have anywhere else.

The problem comes when being on social media stops being a positive or constructive thing. As with any other way of communicating, sometimes you're going to be having laughs a-plenty, and sometimes you're going to get into arguments. Sometimes you're going to talk politics. Sometimes people are going to be mean and awful, because they can hide behind their cartoon profile picture and gripe at you with zero consequences.

If you feel that social media is starting to impact your brain in a negative way, whether that's because you get stuck refreshing in an attempt to get that little brain high again, or because there's just too much information about everything that's going on in the world then it's good to take a step back. How we appear on social

USING YOUR PHONE A LOT DOESN'T MEAN **YOU'RE NOT APPRECIATING LIFE**

media can often become a bit of a performance, because we want to present our best, wittiest selves to the world. And it's *exhausting* to perform that much.

Even if you're having a perfectly nice time on social media it can sometimes be good to hide those apps on your phone in a folder called 'DON'T TOUCH THESE' and live without them for a while. As much as the Internet is great for education and for keeping up with the news, it can actually be nice to have no idea what awful thing has been said or done in the world today.

(As I'm writing this, Donald Trump is sadly the president

of the United States – hopefully by the time you read this we've all been told that this was in fact a dreadful mistake, and he's gone back to just being a regular terrible person. Maybe you're even reading this further in the future and thinking, 'Who's Donald Trump?'. A girl can dream.)

Using your phone a lot doesn't mean you're not appreciating life. I use my phone to learn, speak to my family, connect with friends and strangers online, document the things I don't want to forget, the list goes on ... But even though I think of social media as a positive force in my life, nothing beats the sense of calm I feel when I'm in the countryside and have zero bars of signal. Unless I'm lost in a sheep field.

SHEEP ARE TERRIBLE AT GIVING DIRECTIONS.

I can remove negative people from my online life ...

IF THEY WERE SHOUTING AT ME THROUGH MY WINDOW, I'D CLOSE IT

The Internet is essentially a collection of strangers connected by magic so that they can share pictures of slow lorises and write weird *Great British Bake Off* fanfiction. I'm sure that's not how it was pitched when they were inventing it, but I think that description pretty much covers it.

Being on the Internet doesn't mean there are suddenly different rules for how you can interact with your fellow human, but some people certainly act as if it does. If somebody was standing outside your house in the street shouting, 'You're wrong about politics and your face is very unfortunate!' through your window and you closed it, would that be censorship? Of course not. You'd be completely justified in utilising your window to end that interaction. If somebody followed you around repeatedly being rude to you, it would be a perfectly valid

YOU ARE UNDER NO OBLIGATION TO BE ON **THE RECEIVING END OF INSULTS OR RUDENESS**

choice to get into a taxi and drive away, never to see them again. In fact, you would probably be encouraged to go to the police to report harassment.

You may have heard teachers say that when it comes to something like your lunch break, it's not a right, it's a privilege. It turns out they were extremely wrong about this as when you're an adult, lunch breaks are actually enshrined in employment law and nobody can take them away from you for passing notes to your friends. But it does apply to people on the Internet who demand that they be able to interact with you. You are under no obligation to be on the receiving end of insults or rudeness. You are allowed to block and mute people who think they can flout the rules of common decency just because they're hiding behind the username *harrystyles4evaOK*.

Your social media accounts are what you make of them. If you're of the school of thought that you shouldn't create a bubble for yourself that stops you from seeing the rich tapestry of life, racists and bigots and all, more power to you. But if you want to curate an online existence that doesn't make you want to throw your phone out of the window every time you open Twitter, that's totally allowed!

HARASSMENT AND HATE CRIMES THAT TAKE PLACE ONLINE ARE **JUST AS REAL AS ONES THAT HAPPEN OUT IN THE WORLD**

If bad-temperedness goes one step further and you feel you are being harassed or targeted by people online, you should respond as you would if it were happening in the real world, and take it to the police or other relevant authorities. Unfortunately, systems of authority have been a little bit slow at catching up with things like the Internet, which can leave people unsure about what action is available to them when crimes are taking place online. I'm sure the government initially thought the Internet was a bit of a fad, and not worth spending any time and effort creating pesky new laws for. But harassment and hate crimes that take place online are just as real as ones that happen out in the world, and should be taken seriously.

If you're worried that blocking or unfriending somebody might lead to retaliation, I'd recommend muting or unfollowing them in a way that they won't notice. Features like this are available on most social media sites now and mean that people can be as rude as they like to you and you won't have to see any of it. What's more, you get to experience the smug joy of knowing that they're probably putting time and effort into shouting into the void trying to make you feel bad about your haircut,

AND YOU'LL NEVER, EVER HAVE TO KNOW.

Working towards your dream horse

My first proper job after school was waitressing. I'm the clumsiest person I know – I frequently fall over my own ankles. I've been known to spill a glass of something, absent-mindedly put the half-empty glass down next to me, then spill the rest while cleaning up. On my third week on the job as an events waitress, I was asked to serve red wine to a bride. I was terrified.

The point is, I survived, and having that job helped me learn all about the value of hard work, how to deal with difficult bosses and how to know your own limits. That night I handed the red wine to somebody else, and limited myself to serving clear liquids and eating leftover bread rolls. Education doesn't only happen at school – the world has got a lot to teach you, and not just about the dangers of combining red wine and white dresses.

I am smart in
my own way ...
WHICH MAY ONLY
BECOME OBVIOUS
DURING SPECIFIC
ROUNDS AT A
PUB QUIZ

If you ask me to do some relatively simple maths, I'll immediately reach for my phone calculator or, to my eternal shame, start counting on my fingers like a small child. My brain just doesn't get on with numbers and never has. If you ask me, however, to talk at great length about the themes, motifs and top hotties in Jane Austen novels, you'll never get away. (Bingley is actually the top hottie, FYI.)

Everybody's brain works differently. It's not just that some of us are better at maths and science and others among us (naming no names) feel more at home with the arts. It's about how we perceive the world, and how our brain structures the information it receives. As you may have guessed, I'm no scientist, but actual scientists have studied all the ways our brains differ based on how we're structured and the things we experience.

IT TOOK ME QUITE A LONG TIME TO ACCEPT THE FACT THAT **THERE ARE SOME THINGS I'M NOT NATURALLY PREDISPOSED TO**

It took me quite a long time to accept the fact that there are some things I'm not naturally predisposed to, and probably never will be. I find learning new languages excruciatingly hard. In a fit of pique recently I announced that a universal language should be taught that takes aspects of all the known languages and finds a comfortable middle. And then

I was told that it basically already exists. It's called Esperanto, and when I tried to learn the basics I got just as frustrated as I did with every other language. It's possible ... that *I* might be the problem.

IT CAN BE REALLY EMBARRASSING **WHEN YOUR BRAIN LETS YOU DOWN IN PUBLIC SCENARIOS**

It is frustrating to feel bad at something. And it can be really embarrassing when your brain lets you down in public scenarios. It hurts to be made to feel 'stupid' (a word that's got pretty gross connotations when you think about it) just because you're not queen of algebra, prime minister of politics or the grand high librarian of reading. In those moments, instead of trying to bluff my way through, I like to own the fact that I'm not inhumanly amazing at everything I turn my hand to. Making out that you're better at things than you really are very quickly turns into one of those stressful romcoms where somebody's pretending they're somebody else and waiting to be found out at every turn. Of course they ultimately end up falling in love with the prince they were sent to investigate in the first place, so ... every cloud.

If you shrug and say, 'Actually I'm struggling to work out how much I spent on champagne and mashed potato plus my part of the service charge on this bill – can somebody please do it for me?' I can guarantee you that not a single person you should care about keeping in your life is going to laugh. (At your maths abilities, I mean. They might laugh at you for ordering mashed potato and champagne, but then I'd argue that you also don't want that person in your life.)

The person who helps you out with your potato bill might be the same person who comes to you when they need to write a cover letter and begs you to help them wax poetic about their commitment to fire safety in the workplace, or who calls you up to assemble their IKEA furniture. You might think you're not good at anything in particular, but I can tell you for certain that you're wrong. You might not have a traditional skill, but whether it's how you relate to others, an obscure hobby or even an extremely impressive party trick, you've definitely got something going for you.

Take a second to think about those things. Maybe write them down. Tattoo them on to yourself so you can reach for them whenever necessary and remind yourself of why you're great. I mean a metaphorical tattoo here, not a literal one, or I'd have a list of talents on my bicep that read:

REALITY TV TRIVIA
ENGLISH LITERATURE
OBSCURE POTATO HUMOUR

There's more to life than exam results ...

PEOPLE WILL STILL COME TO YOUR WEDDING IF YOU GET A 'D' IN TEXTILES

I'll always remember a particularly dark time in my life as a secondary school student. For some reason, we all had to take Textiles (possibly a lovely hangover from the past at my all-girls school, preparing us for a life of cross-stitching cushions and saying, 'Yes, dear,' a lot). I was making a cushion for my final project. Yes, a cushion. Most people were making clothes. I was sewing a felt cupcake and some sprinkles on to a couple of squares of fabric. I even had an entire workbook detailing the process. I'd pay to read that again.

I had almost finished my masterpiece – I just had to clear the final hurdles of sewing a few blue and pink beads on to

IT REALLY DID FEEL LIKE THE END OF THE WORLD AT THE TIME. **IT WASN'T**

the icing – when I accidentally left it on a bus. The horror. I was gutted. Not because I'd lost my life's finest work, but because I'd have to start all over again and I was sure I'd run out of time and fail. I lost sleep stressing over this cushion. I clearly didn't think I was destined to have a future in the textiles industry, but I did feel strongly that failing a GCSE wouldn't exactly be a high point for me.

I finished the new cushion just in time, but it was a rush job. The grade I got in the end wasn't great, but it wasn't a fail. And you know what? I can tell you with absolute certainty that it hasn't had any kind of impact on the rest of my life. I had in fact forgotten (or perhaps, repressed) the whole cushion incident until I started thinking about my experiences at school to write this part of the book. It really did feel like the end of the world at the time. It wasn't.

REAL LIFE IS MADE UP OF LOTS OF LITTLE LOW POINTS AND VICTORIES THAT ADD UP TO WHO WE ARE

I had many experiences like this throughout my school career, and even since then in my actual job career there have been moments where I've felt like if I were to be given a grade, a 'D' would be generous. Of course, at the time these things are actually happening, they feel like the end of the world. You can't help but imagine the worst-case scenario consequences for failure. But while obviously you should try your hardest to succeed and do a good job, beating yourself up over exam results, or performance reviews, or synchronised swimming competitions that are already done and dusted isn't healthy.

The way we measure success academically and professionally tends to be very rigid, with no wiggle room to be an actual human being. Real life is made up of lots of little low points and victories that add up to who we are, not one exam one day that determines everything from that point forward. If you're at an age where you're still doing the exams thing, you might think it's easy for me to say this now, with my days of running around in my school kilt (yes, KILT) so long behind me, but one thing I've learned is that there really isn't just one path that's right for you.

Maybe you're a person who thrives academically and will end up with certificates and degrees decorating the walls of your entirely mahogany home office (I don't have any of these, and I'm told that it's not so impressive to do it with your 500- and 1,000-metre swimming certificates). Maybe you're not so academically minded, and you'll decorate your surroundings with your art, or furniture you've made, or photos of your friends and family. Maybe nobody can afford a home office in this economy and all of these hypotheticals are useless to you.

BUT MAYBE NOT!

There are always opportunities to learn ...

THERE'S NO EXCUSE WHEN WE'VE GOT WIKIPEDIA

Do you ever worry that leaving education means that your brain stops gathering new and exciting information and storing it like a hamster stores peanuts? Are you worried that the inside of your head will eventually look like a shrivelled-up raisin or a dry desert with only the occasional dust ball of knowledge or tumbleweed of a fact blowing by? No? Just me?

ARE YOU WORRIED THAT THE INSIDE OF YOUR HEAD WILL EVENTUALLY LOOK LIKE A SHRIVELLED-UP RAISIN?

You're learning all the time as a kid, but when you get a bit older it's easy to go weeks without feeling like you've really internalised any new wisdom. I think we have a tendency to see education and learning as something that only happens in a formal setting like a classroom or lecture hall, or when we crack open intimidating-looking dusty tomes in a library. Not to be so cheesy it hurts (it really does hurt me, I'm very lactose-intolerant) but I have good news! There are many ways to learn, and we're always learning!

I have learned more about politics, social issues, the value of hard work and how to prioritise outside of education than I ever did when I was in it. I'm sure that if you've been out of school for a while, you probably feel the same, or it might be all ahead of you. Living away from home for the first time taught me how to pay bills, make sure a house stays looking like a house rather than looking like the bottom of a handbag (where did all these receipts and food wrappers come from? What's this *sticky thing*?). I learned how to negotiate the politics of living with people who aren't your family without ending up on the news because you've lost it and thrown all their belongings into a pond. These are valuable skills!

IF YOU'RE WORRIED YOUR BRAIN IS TAKING A BIT OF A NAP, **THEN WAKE IT UP!**

From the good old World Wide Web I learned all about activism and critical discussion, and to look outside my own experience and find out how the world's treating everybody else. (Spoiler alert: unless you're afforded the privileges that come with being born in a very lucky set of circumstances, it's often not all that kindly.) I learned that if you've been given a leg-up by life due to your gender, the colour of your skin, your sexual orientation or any number of other factors that can make life that much more breezy, it is your job to amplify the voices of those who haven't, and to work towards a more equal world.

On a slightly less heavy note, you might find that you discover what you're *really* interested in and have more time to devote to that once you're done with education. Having never taken history at school (I was obviously a foolish child who chose making poorly constructed cupcake cushions over learning about the country and world I live in), I now find myself fascinated by it. Spending hours walking around ancient ruins? Cool! Museums full of crumbling relics and that slightly weird smell which I assume is preservative but as a child always thought was blood? Perfect date activity!

If you're worried your brain is taking a bit of a nap, then wake it up! Check some books on ancient Egyptian contraceptive methods out of the library, fall down the Wikipedia hole until you know more than you ever wanted to about the gestation period of an elephant, or visit your local gallery or museum to gaze whimsically at some culture while wearing a beret.

Back in the olden days – don't ask me which olden days, just imagine it's the past and people are wearing top hats in their ordinary lives – knowledge was reserved for the elite. Now pretty much anybody can ask Google why Henry VIII changed the course of history and broke with Rome so that he could get it on with Anne Boleyn,

AND I THINK THAT'S BEAUTIFUL.

I will find
the right path
for me ...

AND WEAR ANKLE
SOCKS AT ALL
TIMES TO PROTECT
MYSELF FROM THE
STINGING NETTLES
OF LIFE

When one door closes, somebody opens a window, almost falls out of it, but grabs on to the curtain at the last minute and stops this from becoming quite a dark way to try to empower you with a life lesson.

When you feel like you've just lost an opportunity or failed, or if you're worried that you haven't made the right choice, it's hard to imagine that what you've missed out on isn't the brightest possible future. Less than ideal exam results, not getting into the university you wanted, job rejections – they make the things you were trying for seem like perfect solutions or outcomes as soon as you can't have them.

CONTRARY TO WHAT PROBIOTIC YOGHURT ADVERTS TRY TO TELL YOU, **THERE IS NO *ONE* WAY TO BE HAPPY**

But there's no way of telling if this future would have actually been the right path for you. Like most things, it probably would have had both positive and negatives, and been nuanced and difficult in ways you can't picture when it's out of reach. We tell ourselves stories about the kind of life we'll have and what we need to get there, so it's hard to deviate from those requirements without feeling a bit glum or afraid.

Contrary to what probiotic yoghurt adverts try to tell you, there is no *one* way to be happy. If everyone derived joy and value from life in the same way as me, the world would be full of professional dog strokers/authors living in tiny but perfectly formed cottages in Scotland, next door to a Nando's. For some people, that probably sounds like hell.

JUST BECAUSE YOU DON'T FEEL COMPLETELY ON TRACK RIGHT NOW, **DOESN'T MEAN YOU'VE SOMEHOW TAKEN A WRONG TURN AND ARE DOOMED TO FAILURE**

Whether you want to be around people, work with animals, solve problems, live in a bustling city or structure your day around dolphin sightings, there are many paths you can take along those lines.

Just because you don't feel completely on track right now, doesn't mean you've somehow taken a wrong turn and are doomed to failure. Although it can feel this way sometimes, your life isn't predetermined, with fate waiting to bring you those inevitable train delays and holiday illnesses. At every stage of life there are opportunities for you to do things a little bit differently.

Ideally (and just to completely contradict the title of this section) we should all stop thinking of education and our careers as irreversible choices that lead us down one set path to our destination. You're not constantly progressing forward to one goal, making big decisions or being graded in a way that will lead you further towards success or send you off on an annoying detour. Our academic and professional lives are actually more like … plants. Hear me out.

Plants are constantly growing new shoots and stalks and stems, bursting off in different directions, and growing out horizontally as well as vertically. They're always reaching towards the sun but also getting what they need from the soil below them, other plants, visiting bees, kindly gardeners, shade, rain and sometimes horse poo. Some plants like to disperse themselves and start growing somewhere else entirely.

When you take a turn you weren't expecting, that's just an offshoot, and sometimes offshoots can grow even taller and produce even more flowers than the original stem. You can still live a great life and you can still bloom, even if you end up somewhere you weren't expecting. This is all getting very whimsical and silly now,

SO I'M PUTTING AN ABRUPT END TO IT.

Happiness can't be bought ...

BUT I WOULD QUITE LIKE A BOAT

money is tricky and I don't know anybody who doesn't have a difficult relationship with it at times. No matter how much you have, you usually want more. The world is constantly trying to sell us things because it's in the interest of companies to make us think that to achieve perfect happiness we must have the world's greatest steam mop, the number one bestselling goldfish obstacle course and Prince Harry's favourite lip balm. Is it any wonder that we often measure our self-worth on how much we, or our families, earn?

I have definitely fallen victim to spending more than I have in an attempt

WE MUST HAVE THE WORLD'S GREATEST STEAM MOP, THE NUMBER ONE BESTSELLING GOLDFISH OBSTACLE COURSE AND PRINCE HARRY'S FAVOURITE LIP BALM

to keep up with others, or even to keep up with my 'ideal' lifestyle. If all your friends are going out to drink fancy drinks and eat tapas it can be difficult to say, 'Actually I can't make it. I'll be at home eating Super Noodles.' This isn't because you're embarrassed about your noodle plan, but because you know which you'd really rather be doing. If you're lucky enough to have a regular income that means you can theoretically keep paying the rent and bills, or buy groceries and occasionally treat yourself, the trick is to accept realistic limits.

There's been a lot of talk of self-care lately. This sounds like a good thing, but unfortunately it has become synonymous with spending money on yourself. Going shopping, buying expensive bath products, getting massages or haircuts are all seen as acts of self-love. Yes, they can be a way of taking care of yourself, but you don't actually have to spend money to do that. I'm sure you've seen enough self-care tips to last you a lifetime, but tough. I'm going to give you some of mine that won't break the bank and therefore your soul:

Get enough sleep (and give yourself ample time to dream about Ryan Gosling or Eva Mendes).

Drink plenty of water. You can get cute little apps that remind you to drink water and reward you for doing it.

Take a bath or a hot shower, regardless of whether or not you budgeted for a bath bomb this month. When I'm clean I feel like a whole new person – peppy and go-getting and a bit like a young female lawyer in a noughties romcom who's about to take on the world with just a positive attitude and a flip phone.

Put on clean clothes. If I stay in the same clothes or in pyjamas for too long I turn into a slug person. If I feel sluggy, I act sluggy, drooling ooze everywhere and being at constant risk of being stepped on (emotionally). But

when I have clean clothes on? I refer you back to the aforementioned young female lawyer persona.

Watch or listen to something comforting and familiar, like a TV show you know off by heart. It also helps a lot if you wrap yourself in blankets/build some sort of soft furnishing fort and then watch from your human cocoon.

Ask somebody nice if they'll brush your hair, or do your make-up/nails, or otherwise give you a little bit of physical pampering. Ideally someone you know, not just someone in the street who looks like they're not awful. A lot of the luxurious self-care stuff to do with hitting the spa or getting a manicure is really about having somebody take care over doing something platonically lovely for you, and it can be much nicer, in fact, if it's a mate rather than Brunette Sandra down at Pure Massage.

There's nothing wrong with spending money on yourself – you shouldn't be ashamed of splashing out occasionally if you're able to. But studies have shown that past a certain financial threshold, people's quality of life doesn't actually improve by having more money. It's very possible to treat yourself without spending a penny, and at the risk of sounding like a knob, some of the best things in life really are free. That's what I like to hold on to, anyway, whenever I'm wondering

IF I CAN BUDGET FOR A DESIGNER CAT COLLAR THIS MONTH.

I will curate a
life full of
things I love ...

NOT THE THINGS
BEAUTY BLOGGERS
TELL ME TO LOVE

Have you ever been mocked for not owning the right brand of *thing*? This doesn't happen so much now that I'm a grown-up, but when I was younger I remember being mercilessly teased for having the wrong school shoes (far too sensible), uncool gel pens (unscented) and distinctly unglamorous hair (I dyed a white blonde streak at the front of it to try to combat this problem but, retrospectively, I suspect I made it worse).

It's drilled into us from a young age that some items are better and more worth having than others. This isn't always based on being more expensive; sometimes the 'right' thing is just having the

THERE'S ALWAYS SOMETHING EXPENSIVE **THAT WE'RE SUPPOSED TO ASPIRE TO OWN**

proper colour shag bands (only Google these if you want to be slightly horrified about how we talked about them when we were eight), but quite often it is to do with being a brand.

This is great for brands, who get to cash in on this cultural currency when kids, teenagers and adults shell out for a name stamped on something 'Made in China'. But not so great if you or your family can't afford or refuse to engage with those brand names. When you're a kid this might be about a brand of pencil case, but as you get older it's often about clothing, cars, designer water purifiers, etc.

There's always something expensive that we're supposed to aspire to own. It's meant to be a sign of status, taste and wealth to have something that can be instantly recognised as fancy, like a gold-plated smoothie-maker or those cool shoes that have pop-out wheels to become roller skates (but the wheels are encrusted with diamonds!). When you're bombarded with imagery of wealth, or the impression of wealth – especially as social media makes it so easy to watch the Kardashians unbox 100 pairs of designer shoes on a random Tuesday – it's hard not to buy into the culture and start wanting the shiny things.

IT'S HARD NOT TO BUY INTO THE CULTURE AND START WANTING THE SHINY THINGS

If you have the means to make big purchases and that's really what you want, then knock yourself out – I'm definitely not immune to this phenomenon! But it sucks that we're often made to feel lesser if we can't afford or justify getting the flashiest stuff. There's a big class issue at play here, because when you're blasted with imagery of what it means to have a happy life, and it tends to involve spending a lot of money, of course you're going to feel inferior or unworthy if it seems really out of reach. There can be a lot of grim, snobbish mockery of 'working class' people who buy expensive brands, but if these things are seen as symbols of personal and professional success, then of course we're all going to covet them.

The thing to focus on is what makes you *genuinely* happy, rather than what you think you should own because other people do. You might have a jumper that's been in your wardrobe for ten years that you put on every time you feel sad and need to be a bit cosier than usual, and that's probably far more valuable to you than a designer one that you only pull out for special occasions in case you spill spaghetti sauce on it.

Things that make us feel good, that are associated with great people and memories, that help us express who we are as people and that are genuinely useful in our day-to-day lives should be the things that we hold on to and cherish. There might be a bit of crossover, but I think most of the stuff bought because of peer pressure, to be cool, or because we saw a Kardashian modelling one,

IS PROBABLY GOING TO END UP IN A CHARITY SHOP RATHER THAN AS A TREASURED POSSESSION.

My job does not define me ...

IT'S JUST WHAT I'M DOING RIGHT NOW SO THAT I CAN AFFORD BISCUITS

When you were a kid (assuming you were a kid, and weren't manifested by witches as a full-grown person) what did you want to be when you grew up? All of my dreams revolved around getting as much attention as possible. This may have been the case because my younger sister was far cuter than me. She looked like an actual painting of a cherub, all chubby cheeks and blonde curls, and I looked a bit like a rat in a bowl-cut wig.

I wanted to be a famous actress, or a famous author, or a singer. I used to write very terrible books in felt tip pen and my most memorable was called, *Oh No, Not Camping!* I

I OFTEN USED TO SING AT HOME WITH THE WINDOWS OPEN IN THE HOPE THAT A TALENT MANAGER MIGHT WALK PAST

had never even been camping. I often used to sing at home with the windows open in the hope that a talent manager might walk past, hear me and immediately want to sign me to a label and start recording my first album.

Sadly, most of us don't end up doing the job we wanted when we were kids. Often that's because we grow out of those dreams and get new ones, or possibly because there's no such thing as being an underwater police cowboy (YET).

Our new dreams are usually a bit more attainable, which is why it's so hard when we feel like what we're doing for work isn't part of that dream. It's a difficult time to be a young person in the world (or a middle-aged person, or an older person – basically anybody who's not bringing in the megabucks or inheriting millions from their family's cactus shop fortune)

YOUR LIFE DOESN'T HAVE TO BE
ALL OR NOTHING

and it's very normal to be doing a job that's nothing like the job you truly want.

I don't know about you, but when it dawned on me that you really do only get one life, and one lifetime's worth of chances to find jobs and a path that works for you, I had a huge freak-out, ate a whole saucepan of mashed potato and didn't sleep for a week. I really hope that reading that last sentence hasn't been the cause of that realisation for you right now, because there isn't a huge market for books that cause deep, existential dread, and it probably makes you no longer eligible for the Nobel Peace Prize for self-help books. Anyway, that realisation can be a bit scary, especially if you feel like you're quite far away from achieving your dreams.

A lesson I've learned (and I hope it will help you feel less like inhaling mashed potato right now) is that there are lots of different ways to have a good life. If you have a job that you're not thrilled about but you have good friends at that job, or it's teaching you some valuable skills, that's not by any means a bad situation to be in. If your job sucks but you've accepted it as a necessity so that you can manage expenses, eat crisps and generally be a person, that's okay too. Your life outside your job, your relationships with friends and loved ones, your hobbies, the things you choose for yourself rather than do out of necessity, are the things that really define you.

Just because you aren't the world's sexiest astronaut or a professional Monopoly player doesn't mean those dreams can't be part of your life. If you love space, you can set up a space-themed blog, or pitch articles to *All About Space* magazine, or go and hear talks from astronomers and real astronauts. If you're all about Monopoly, you could start a Monopoly podcast, form a Monopoly players' society in your area, meet other Monopoly fiends and make friends for life after bonding over Bond Street. Your life doesn't have to be all or nothing. You should definitely go after your dreams of course, but if you find your dream-to-practicalities ratio ends up at about forty-sixty,

THAT'S A PRETTY NICE LIFE TO HAVE.

I fully commit
to anything
I do ...

FROM SPREADSHEETS
TO WORLD
DOMINATION

I'm always surprised at the power of my brain. No, not because I can so readily reel off the names of all the Kardashians, the Kardashian-Jenners and their various children, but because I've realised that I can basically trick myself into feeling differently about certain aspects of my life! We have natural responses to lots of things: scary things make us jump, boring things make us yawn and Adam Sandler films make us realise cinema tickets are too expensive these days to take a risk on a film.

You can build up negative associations to things you used to be totally chill with due to one bad experience. You can also feel good about something you used to feel rubbish about through positive reinforcement. This is important, because when you have mastery over your brain you can make yourself feel good about things you have to do out of necessity – like going to work or school.

SCRUB THE GROUT LIKE IT'S **YOUR AUDITION PERFORMANCE FOR *X FACTOR***

Sadly I don't have a magic trick that's going to make you instantly fall in love with your job and skip to work singing with the pigeons and the squirrels like an off-brand Disney character, but it's such a shame to feel *meh* about work when most of us spend at least thirty-five hours a week at our desks/tills/undercover sting operations.

Take putting numbers in a spreadsheet as an example. I'm not saying that it's ever going to be a thrilling, laugh-a-minute jaunt you'll remember for years to come. But if you absolutely smash it out of the park, inputting everything in half a day, triple-checking it and sending it over before the deadline so you can get a head start on tomorrow's work, you're going to feel pretty great about yourself. No matter what the work is, you can find a way to do it well and feel satisfied at the end of the day.

SADLY I DON'T HAVE A MAGIC TRICK THAT'S GOING TO MAKE YOU INSTANTLY FALL IN LOVE WITH YOUR JOB AND SKIP TO WORK SINGING WITH THE PIGEONS

It's easier said than done, but approaching as much of your life as possible with enthusiasm helps you rewire your brain to feel positive about getting all sorts of things done. Try approaching something work- or life-related that you usually see as a chore with the attitude that this is a task you can ace, rather than just get through. Skip to the recycling bins in record time. Send that email with great aplomb. Scrub the grout like it's your audition performance for *X Factor*. With time, you might be able to feel this way about lots of things in life that you dread or put off.

Of course, there'll always be those days or moments when you're really just not feeling it, and that's okay. It'll balance out the rest of the time when you

QUEEN OF THE SPREADSHEETS!
KING OF EMAILS!

feel like you're being the best you can be at whatever you do. Queen of the spreadsheets! King of emails! Duchess of listening enthusiastically to your boss while they tell you dull gardening stories!

EVERY LITTLE KID'S DREAM.

My soul belongs to me, not my boss ...

WAIT, ACTUALLY I SOLD IT IN 2011 FOR TAYLOR SWIFT TICKETS

*Y*ou get to pick your friends, but you don't get to choose your family, and you certainly don't get to choose your colleagues (unless you're lucky enough to have some mates on the hiring committee).

Your workplace is weird because you do spend quite a lot of your life there. You'll see the people you work closely with much more than you'll ever see your best friends, and yet you're unlikely to ask Janet in marketing for her advice about how to break up with someone via text, or Cyril from accounts if he's got a spare pair of pants because you had a tiny accident in yours while watching a very funny YouTube video of a cat falling off a table.

Generally in life, if you

IT'S ESPECIALLY DIFFICULT IF THE PERSON YOU DON'T GET ON WITH **HAPPENS TO BE YOUR BOSS**

don't get on with someone or you don't enjoy the vibe somewhere you can go to great lengths to avoid them. But at work, it would probably end in a HR bullying tribunal if you were to get up and leave the room mid-sentence and mid-meeting every time the person you didn't get on with walked in.

It's especially difficult if the person you don't get on with happens to be your boss. Bosses wield a certain amount of power over you, and while mostly this is fine and they understand that great power comes with great responsibility (thanks *Spider-Man*), sometimes power corrupts (thanks Lord John Acton, the prominent nineteenth-century political figure who's associated with popularising that phrase).

I find that the easiest way to get through tough work situations is not to take any criticism personally. Of course, if you feel like you're actually being bullied or discriminated by a colleague or manager you should definitely speak to your HR department. But if you just find people a bit difficult to work with, or it's not your ideal working atmosphere, it's a case of separating your job from the rest of your life in your brain.

This might not make you feel like employee of the year, but

WORK DOESN'T HAVE TO BE **A HORRIBLE, HARD SLOG**

the truth is that you're only paid to be at work a certain number of hours of the day (unless you get paid for your overtime, which most of us don't), and it is a good and healthy thing to leave the office once those hours are done. It is also a good and healthy thing to take your entire lunch hour, to march about the shops, chill out in a café or share your sandwich with some swans. Aside from having far too much work to do, leaving when your hours are up can also be very hard because of the disapproving glares you get from Janet and Cyril. When this happens, grit your teeth and think, *Stare all you want, pals – I've got a life outside the office worth going home for.*

Work doesn't have to be a horrible, hard slog, but you also

don't have to pretend to anybody that you love your job so much that you'd be there even if you weren't being paid. 'No, really! I just love serving people food/coding spreadsheets/ writing press releases! I often wander about the streets, trying to hand strangers cups of coffee/do taxes/promote the latest model of steam mop!' You are being paid to do a job until you aren't. And at that point, with as much dignity as you can muster, gather your things and

RUN FOR THE HILLS.

The world is my shiny oyster

How do you feel the world is doing right now? If it had a Yelp page, what kind of review would you leave?

3*, NOT EXACTLY A LUXURY EXPERIENCE BUT IT DID THE TRICK. MANAGERS ALL KEPT ARGUING AMONG THEMSELVES, BUT THERE ARE SOME VERY NICE VOLCANOES AND BEACHES.

Things might be looking a bit dire right now when it comes to politics and the global situation, but all is not lost. If you want to give the world a boost so it starts getting those elusive five stars, you need to work out what you want it to look like and how you can help to achieve that – and then get stuck in.

There is more
good than bad
in this world ...

AND SOMETIMES
THERE ARE
POTATO WAFFLES

I'm writing this a little while before you'll get to read it, and I really hope that the world is looking a bit brighter over there in the future. Maybe by the time you're seeing these words, we'll have invented hover cars, nailed gender equality and somehow mixed cats and dogs together to form the perfect animal – wait, that's basically foxes. It's already been done. It's foxes, everybody.

WE CAN'T JUST WALK AROUND **EXPECTING GOOD THINGS**

It does seem like the world has been getting worse lately. I doubt this is true – it probably felt a bit more terrible back when the Great Plague was happening. But now we have instant access to every bad thing that happens through the magic of technology. If there had been smartphones in the 1300s, I'm sure that the Black Death would have seemed that much more depressing, with daily headlines such as, 'Forty per cent of English Population Now Dead', 'King Edward III Spotted Golfing' and 'Ten Ways You Can Style Out Your Buboes'. (Buboes, which the bubonic plague was named after, are swollen lymph glands. You learn something new every day!)

Thinking about all the times in the past when things have been just as bad may seem gloomy, but it might offer a little perspective and make you realise that in most ways, the experience of being human isn't actually in steady decline – there have been lots of ups and downs throughout history when things probably felt every bit as dire. Of course, there's a chance that thinking about all the bad things that have ever happened might not perk you up, and I don't really blame you.

SOMETHING GOOD IS HAPPENING RIGHT NOW. AND NOW. AND NOW. YOU GET THE POINT.

To look at it another way (a way that hopefully won't make you want to build a cave out of books, pronounce yourself king and refuse to ever come out), the major news outlets don't tend to report on all the good things that are happening around us. It's not interesting or profitable to talk about the nice things that make life worth living. Every day there are hundreds of thousands, nay, MILLIONS, of excellent interactions and experiences going on around the globe. Something good is happening right now. And now. And now. You get the point.

Luckily for us, people *have* actually started going out of their way to publicise the good as well as the bad to keep us all slightly saner. You can easily find positive stories from around the world if you look for them – there are even entire websites dedicated to telling stories about progress and hope. I'm not saying that you should stick your head in the sand and pretend that famine, corruption and endless superhero film sequels aren't happening, but you can try to maintain some balance and perspective with what you consume.

Of course, you can also help to tip the balance yourself. We can't just walk around expecting good things, like sports victories, political progress and elderly sausage dogs in little coats, to fall into our laps without putting anything good out there ourselves. I don't really believe in karma, but I do believe that being positive leads to positive things. Even if it doesn't change how life treats you, it changes how you feel about life, and honestly that can be half the battle.

Try being actively nice to people who work in retail instead of just staring at your debit card awkwardly while they ring up your slipper socks, or offering to do a friend a favour when you know they're struggling, or even doing a bit of charity or political volunteering to contribute to creating the kind of world you want to live in.

You can be a force for good in the world! What a great thing to be able to do. You might not be like the group of elephants in that adorable video, saving their elephant son from a swamp, but you'll still be doing something amazing,

AND THAT'S WHAT REALLY MATTERS.

I will be
thoughtful about
my impact on
the world ...

SO I DON'T HAVE TO
BOOK MYSELF ON
THE FIRST SHUTTLE
TO MARS

We only have one Earth, and although we're making grand plans to jet off to new planets and start fun new colonies where nobody can go outside or ever come back if they get a bit homesick (yay – such fun!), it seems sensible for us to try to hold on to what we've already got and make it as sustainable as possible for future generations of our grandchildren, holographic children, robot children, etc.

The problem is that our desire to innovate quickly, live convenient and comfortable lives and to have lots of material things available almost instantly to us is impacting the planet. I don't want to be a huge downer, but it's pretty well known at this point that we're:

a) burning a lot of fossil fuels
b) creating a lot of waste
c) using unsustainable business practices and exploiting workers in the process of a) and b)

I doubt you're the president of a big oil company or the CEO of a fast fashion label, but you probably are a consumer (unless you've nailed life and live in a beautiful eco-hut you built with your own hands, eating oddly shaped carrots that you've grown in your victory garden, and use winning smiles as currency). Being a consumer means that you make certain choices every day about how to spend your money. Unfortunately for a lot of us, the cheaper or more convenient route when it comes to things like transport or buying clothes and food is often the only

THERE ARE LOTS OF LITTLE CHANGES YOU CAN MAKE IN YOUR LIFE **TO BE NICE TO THE PLANET**

one available. This is nothing to be ashamed of. You didn't make it so that super-ethical living is often only accessible for people earning quite a bit of cash! The best that we can do is try to be thoughtful consumers with whatever resources we have available to us.

There are lots of little changes you can make in your life to be nice to the planet. Here are some that I've found easiest to incorporate into my daily human existence:

Using less single-use plastic

It's definitely a tricky one because so many things come pre-packaged with enough plastic to laminate every page of the *Lord of the Rings* books, but looking out for alternatives and shopping at markets can help reduce the amount you purchase.

Recycling everything you possibly can

Cans, cardboard, fabric, chat-up lines – you name it, it can probably be recycled at your local community refuse point.

Getting a reusable mug for hot drinks

… and a reusable water bottle for … well, I hope I don't have to explain what it's for. Coffee shops will happily fill up your travel mug, and as disposable coffee cups can't be recycled

(I felt personally betrayed when I found out I'd been chucking them into the recycling bin fruitlessly for years), they're a must.

Shopping for clothes less often

… and trying to visit charity and vintage shops when you do. Fast fashion is a bit of an ethical nightmare, and although it's much easier to pop into your local high street chain to pick something up for the weekend, the pure satisfaction of finding the perfect vintage fringed cowboy jacket for a tenner in a Cancer Research UK shop is truly glorious.

Choosing cruelty-free options

The day I found out that almost all high street make-up and skincare is tested on animals, I felt like I'd fallen into a parallel universe in a dystopian young adult novel. Unfortunately, I hadn't and it's all very real. But there are handy lists online that tell you what's cruelty-free, so you can arm yourself with knowledge next time you go shopping.

Aside from personal changes like these, if you're thinking about becoming a tree-hugging do-gooder then there are plenty of activist and charity campaigns aimed at the companies who produce plastic, fast fashion, mountains of coffee cups and so on. Get involved, get active and put down that application form for the first Mars shuttle.

WE'RE STAYING HERE, FOLKS!

I will use
my privilege to
help others ...

**THERE ARE HARDLY
ANY 'I'S IN 'LEVEL
PLAYING FIELD'**

This is a difficult subject to talk about, because I'm coming at it from a position of privilege, and that means there are lots of things I can never fully understand. I encourage you to do as much research as possible into what privilege you have – whether because you're white, straight, cisgender, male, able-bodied or your parents own three houses.

A GOOD PLACE TO START IS TO **STOP TALKING AND START LISTENING**

I understand why being called 'privileged' can cause a knee-jerk reaction, because if you feel that life hasn't always been kind to you or you've been disadvantaged in some ways, that label might not feel like it fits. But privilege is inherent because of how society is structured, and it's not an attack to say that some people benefit from that structure more than others – it's just an unfortunate fact of life.

Privilege is complicated but it boils down to this: if there are inherent things about you that mean you get preferential treatment, or a leg-up in life, or simply don't experience discrimination in the ways that other people do, then you're benefitting from it. If you've never had someone side-eye you in a shop because of the colour of your skin, you are privileged. If you've never had someone assume you can't work in a position of power because of your gender, that's privilege too. If you've never struggled to navigate a public transport system because it wasn't built for your body, guess what? Privilege all over the show.

It's possible to be privileged in some ways and disadvantaged in others. You might be a cisgender, white, able-bodied gay man, and therefore experience discrimination for your sexuality. If you have any privilege at all, I think it's important to try to use it to make the world better for everybody. A good place to start is to stop talking and start listening. Everything I'm discussing right now I have learned from zipping these lips and paying attention to what people who don't have the same privileges as me are saying and trying to achieve (rather than what I assume they want).

IT'S IMPORTANT TO ACCEPT **THAT YOU'RE ALWAYS LEARNING**

There is a tendency for privileged people to speak over others without realising it. This is often well-meaning – we're trying to share information and tell stories with the aim of achieving progress that helps people. But if they're not our stories to tell, then by doing this we're only contributing to the idea that our voices are the ones that matter. Instead, share content from the people who actually experience the discrimination you're trying to end.

No matter how much you think you're a good 'ally' – a word that some people like to wear as a badge of honour even when it hasn't been earned – it's important to accept that you're always learning. There's no moment where you'll suddenly understand every facet of inequality and how to solve it. You should always be open to the idea that there's more education to be had.

Another thing to always keep in mind is that it's not enough to only stand up to injustice when it's convenient. If you're privileged, you're benefitting from imbalance, and discrimination might not affect you on a daily basis. This means that inequality might not always be at the forefront of your brain – something that is impossible for people who are disadvantaged by it.

WORK OUT HOW YOU CAN USE THE ADVANTAGES YOU'VE BEEN GIVEN IN LIFE TO HELP OTHER PEOPLE

I know that we all have our own nonsense going on, and I'm not saying that you absolutely have to become a full-time activist and quit your regular life to paint quippy yet inspirational protest banners. But if you care about a more equal world, and I think everybody should, work out how you can use the advantages you've been given in life to help other people, and try to make it part of how you live.

I apologise for the unusually serious tone in this section. Sometimes – very rarely, but sometimes –

THERE ARE THINGS TOO IMPORTANT TO MAKE DOG JOKES ABOUT.

I will engage
with politics
to build a
better future ...

AND INCREASE
THE AMOUNT OF
POLITICAL DEBATES
I START AT PARTIES

*O*ur lives are in the hands of politicians. I know it's pretty gross to think about, as lots of politicians are old white dudes who spend £14,000 a year of our tax money on luxury skateboards for their dogs. But politics really does have a huge impact on our daily lives and the lives of those around us, so the obvious conclusion is that we need to be politically involved if we want to have a say in our own futures.

Young people have a track record of being relatively bad at voting. Any time politicians talk about lowering the voting age or engaging the youths

IF YOU'RE NOT INVOLVED, THEN OTHER PEOPLE ARE ESSENTIALLY **MAKING ALL YOUR DECISIONS FOR YOU**

using these things called 'gifs' and 'memes', people argue that it's a waste of time, because young people just don't care about politics. But this is definitely changing – people are able to educate themselves online, find communities of people who are discussing politics from an early age, and see the real impact political decisions have on other people's lives.

I strongly believe that it's important to work out where you stand when it comes to politics and to vote at every opportunity. If you're not involved, then other people are essentially making all your decisions for you. No matter how apathetic you might feel about the often mediocre buffet of politicians that seems to be on offer, if you don't make a choice, somebody else chooses and you end up with a plateful of cottage cheese and some dry pickles. I'm sorry, I couldn't think of bad realistic buffet food. In my eyes, everything you can eat at a buffet is a gift.

Work out which political parties you genuinely think are best for your country and for championing the things you care about, and try to ignore the petty political fighting as much as you can (tuning in to Prime Minister's Questions on TV is like watching a pond full of goldfish in a feeding frenzy, except that all the goldfish are screaming) and ensure you make your voice count.

Try not to get too sucked into spending hours arguing with people who won't stop calling you a 'snowflake' on the Internet, or to get into too many screaming rows with relatives during family occasions. But don't feel that you need to keep your views quiet, either – discussing your worldview and having it challenged is an important part of forming who you are and what you believe.

IT'S EASY TO FEEL THAT WE DON'T HAVE MUCH INFLUENCE ON **THE WAY THINGS ARE RUN**

It's easy to feel that we don't have much influence on the way things are run. But this isn't actually true, and lots of politicians and their skateboarding dogs are relying on you to think this way so that, like *Scooby-Doo* villains, they can crack on with their own agenda without being thwarted by meddling kids.

Whether it's involvement through local or general elections, campaigning, debate or card-holding party membership, make sure you know where you stand and how you think we can make the world a better place.

I'D SUGGEST MORE
ALL-YOU-CAN-EAT BUFFETS,
TO START.

It is not my responsibility to fix everything ...

I AM JUST ONE PERSON AND HAVE NOT BEEN BITTEN BY A RADIOACTIVE OVER-ACHIEVER

I've talked a lot in this book about the things you can do to improve your life, or to improve other people's lives, or to try to help save this beautiful planet we call the Bluey-Green Space Marble (I'm sure loads of people definitely call it that). While I think all of this is valid (it would be quite unfortunate if I didn't, having written it), I also think there's a

IT'S NOT YOUR JOB TO SOLVE **ALL THE WORLD'S PROBLEMS**

lot of value in realising that it's not your job to solve all the world's problems, or your friends' problems, or even your own problems.

Taking on all these things at once is exhausting. Once you open the Pandora's Box of caring about things, it's impossible to put the lid back on, and you might end up feeling very overwhelmed by a desire to do good in the world, be a great friend, achieve a blissful state of self-love and still have time to binge-watch *Keeping Up with the Kardashians* at the weekend.

You're no good to humankind if you're so stressed out by all the things you want to fix and change that you can't even begin to do one of them, and end up sitting in your dressing gown eating dry cereal from a box and telling your cat that it's pointless to even try because there's just too much to do.

If there are things you can feasibly do to help make the world a better place, I think you should do them. I think even small changes to how you relate to other people, how you shop and how you think about yourself can have really big impacts. HOWEVER, I also think that you should never feel guilty or beat yourself up about having limits as a person, or sometimes needing to become an unproductive but very happy slug-person in your bed all weekend, or even about sometimes making decisions that put you first and the greater good second.

An example of this that I often struggle with is that when it comes to trying to be charitable or an activist, there seem to be so many problems that I don't know where to start. Instead I end up freezing and doing nothing because there are too many decisions to be made. It is impossible to help everyone and every cause, so you have to pick a few things that are important to you and leave the rest for another time, or even for other people to crack on with. Choose improving literacy, or fighting malaria, or

YOU SHOULD NEVER FEEL GUILTY OR BEAT YOURSELF UP ABOUT HAVING LIMITS AS A PERSON

a business that 3D-prints prosthetic feet for London pigeons (this charity doesn't exist yet, but if I can just get my hands on a 3D printer and tens of thousands of the footless pigeons that limp the city streets, I'll be in business).

This logic has to apply to everything else in your life too. You are only one human being! Don't put so much pressure on yourself that caring about things becomes a burden rather than something that gives you drive and hope for the future. You will have plenty of opportunities in your life to do good and effect change, and burning yourself out early so that you become like the cynical older character in an epic film who has become so jaded that they don't care about the cause any more isn't helpful to anyone.

DO WHAT YOU CAN, BUT DO NO MORE AND NO LESS

Do what you can, but do no more and no less.

AND IF YOU'RE INTERESTED IN HELPING OUT WITH A PROSTHETIC PIGEON FEET CHARITY, HIT ME UP.

I will live by
my beliefs ...

AS MUCH AS IS
POSSIBLE WITHOUT
BECOMING A CAVE
HERMIT

We all have grand ideas about how the world and the people in it should be and behave. I, for example, think that we should cede power to the dogs and let them decide how things should be run. I can't wait to destroy all the important historical landmarks and rebuild them out of bits of bacon, held together with peanut butter.

The problem comes when we actually try to live by our beliefs. It turns out that it's easy to think that we shouldn't exploit anybody, that we should look after the planet or that eating lots of meat probably isn't the best idea, but much harder to follow through with choices that put those beliefs into action.

I am not trying to guilt you into changing the way you live your life here, because I think it's a real shame that lots of people and organisations

I DON'T FIND GUILT TO BE A PARTICULARLY **HEALTHY MOTIVATOR**

have come to rely on guilt as a tactic to get people on board with them. It's not that there aren't things we should feel guilty for, because of course there's lots of bad in the world thanks to human beings – but I don't find guilt to be a particularly healthy motivator, and I'm sure you don't either.

There's a lot of feeling that if you don't do things 100 per cent – if you don't become a perfect level 9,000 vegan who makes their own hummus and levitates slightly off the ground at all times, if you don't quit buying clothes and start sewing your own out of old pillowcases like Dobby the house elf, if you don't start making your own moisturiser out of olive oil and good intentions – you've somehow failed or can't be part of the movement.

This, of course, is nonsense. It's not that you must make every possible change to your lifestyle to make the world better or you have no effect at all. If you want to eat less meat and therefore decide to go meat-free during the week, or if you start browsing charity shops for non-urgent shopping only nipping to Topshop when you need an outfit at short notice, those things will have impact.

It's not a case of only bothering about these things when they're convenient, but of being realistic about what you can achieve with the time and resources that you have available to you. Often having the freedom to be able to make these choices is linked to privilege. People who wear larger clothes sizes, for example, can really struggle to shop second-hand, so don't feel bad if you feel you can't achieve perfect eco-god or goddess efficiency right now.

I often speak to people who say that they believe certain things are right but that they're too set in their ways to change. This is also nonsense. It's never too late to make a change! You might need a bit more willpower and support but I genuinely do believe that living more closely aligned with your core beliefs leads to feeling a lot more satisfied about how you've spent your time on Earth.

IT'S NEVER TOO LATE TO MAKE A CHANGE!

Activism is closely tied with negative reinforcement – showing people the terrible things that are going on, using guilt to try to get them to care and get involved. Sometimes I'm sure this does work but I'd rather we talked about the good bits. What would we like to achieve through positive change? Let's stop trying to make people feel bad for living the way they've been taught by society up until now.

So please pick some things you care about and work out how you could apply these beliefs to your life (if you're not already). But please don't feel bad for not being perfect, and ignore anybody who tries to make you feel that way. Nobody's perfect.

WE'VE ALL ACCIDENTALLY CLICKED ON A *DAILY MAIL* LINK AT SOME POINT.

Goodbye!

You've finished reading this book! Has your entire life changed dramatically beyond recognition? Can you say that on tape, so that I have proof and can put it on the cover?

I hope that it has been helpful for you, and that you feel better equipped to deal with some of the nonsense life throws your way. Or failing that, that you occasionally did a sort of half-laugh out loud or chuckled quietly on the inside at some of my terrible jokes.

I'm not an expert in anything, as I'm sure you've gathered by now, so I wanted to make sure that you have somewhere to go next if you need proper resources for anything that I've touched on in this book. Please do take a look in the front of the book if you feel you need a bit more help than what you got from my ramblings, and I hope you face the rest of your day, week, or maybe your WHOLE LIFE (all right, I could sense that I was taking it a step too far but it was worth a try) with new ways of thinking about the challenges you meet.

Lex Croucher

Lex is one of the UK's leading female YouTubers with over fifteen million views and more than 125,000 subscribers on her YouTube channel. With ten years of making online content under her belt, she currently creates comedy and lifestyle content with a particular focus on gender, political activism, ethical fashion and beauty, mental health and feminism. She also co-hosts the romantic advice podcast *Make Out With Him*. Lex is an advocate for self-empowerment, independence and always being able to laugh at yourself.

Lex co-founded the 'Women on YouTube' panel at VidCon and is committed to using her platform to help and support women and girls. She believes in the power of YouTube and social media to publicise causes and achieve positive change in the world. In particular Lex is passionate about the importance of having women properly represented online and counteracting the sexism and abuse that so many women face on the internet.

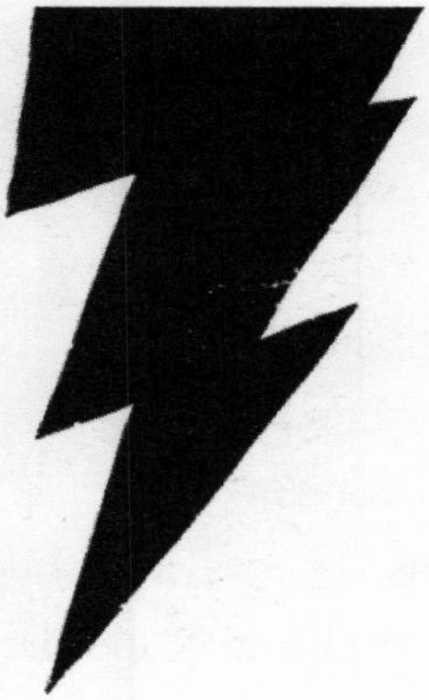